# The CHOSEN
## appetizers & desserts

birmingham alabama what's cooking in birmingham phoenix arizona eat and
pepper to taste berkeley california the berkeley jewish cookbook beverly hills
beverly hills california from noodles to strudles castro valley california what's c
california flavored with love palo alto california favorite recipes san diego cali
california delectable collectab'⸺ ⸺da second helpings, please! r
health stamford connectic⸺ ⸺hartford connecticut pass⸺
leavened with love clear⸺ ⸺aytona beach florida m
florida food for thoug⸺ ⸺vorite recipes balabu
hallandale florida d⸺ ⸺ily favorites hollyw
gourmet delights⸺ ⸺ksonville florida tr
this and kosher t⸺ ⸺allahassee floric
jewish dishes a'⸺ ⸺appy cooker a
kitchen chicag⸺ ⸺the fort sheri
cookbook wil⸺ ⸺a the cooker
recipes dave⸺ ⸺na kitchen t
louisiana fr⸺ ⸺ook potom⸺
massachus⸺ ⸺ought coc
center tab'⸺ ⸺abody ma
sudbury n⸺ ⸺ts the hap
arbor mic⸺ ⸺e mama ι
magic oa'⸺ ⸺e afraid t⸺
treats col⸺ ⸺neration
council's⸺ ⸺garden
inois wo⸺ ⸺kery ce⸺
va specia⸺ ⸺en treat⸺
essen 'n⸺ ⸺sey to se
jersey lo⸺ ⸺on new j
new mex⸺ ⸺ew york
bingham⸺ ⸺s brookl⸺
kosher je⸺ ⸺new yor
new york t.⸺ ⸺om our be⸺
elegant es⸺ ⸺om dora w
enjoy malv⸺ ⸺itchen ma⸺
inspirations⸺ ⸺ew york new
plainview ne⸺ ⸺k favorite re⸺
hadassah coo.⸺ ⸺ring valley ne⸺
island new yor⸺ ⸺s choice west l
spice charlotte r.⸺ ⸺favorite recipe⸺
cleveland ohio fa⸺ ⸺e sport of cookir⸺
kitchen cincinnati c⸺ ⸺chef bala cynwyd p
havertown pennslyva.⸺ ⸺ylvania plotz and pan
with love philadelphia ι⸺ ⸺terhood cookbook stat
women of brit shalom wyι⸺ ⸺ck and easy cookbook cha
charleston with love charlesto⸺. ⸺istorically speaking columbia
blountville tennessee recipes by request oryan texas favorite recipes dallas te⸺
arthur texas bicentennial cookbook danville virginia favorite recipes from our
from soup to nosh lynchburg virginia kitchen knishes newport news virginia a
virginia try it you'll like it parkersburg west virginia season to taste milwaukee w

# The CHOSEN
# appetizers & desserts

edited by Marilyn Stone
illustrated by Lea Gabbay

THE CHOSEN
COOKBOOK SERIES

TRIAD PUBLISHING COMPANY     GAINESVILLE, FLORIDA

**Library of Congress Cataloging in Publication Data**

Main entry under title:
The Chosen, appetizers & desserts.

Includes index.
1. Cookery (Appetizers)   2. Desserts.   3. Cookery, Jewish
I. Stone, Marilyn.   II. Title: Chosen, appetizers and desserts.
TX740.C44      641.8'6      82-2836
ISBN 0-937404-11-X (plastic comb)     AACR2
ISBN 0-937404-10-1 (pbk.)

Published and distributed by Triad Publishing Company, Inc.
P.O. Box 13096, Gainesville, Florida 32604

# Preface

More than two years ago, the Sisterhood of B'nai Israel Congregation began collecting recipes from the fundraising cookbooks of other Jewish organizations, with the ambitious plan of publishing the best recipes we could find. After all, we reasoned, if each book contains its members' best, we would have something truly spectacular, a "best of the best."

It didn't take long, however, to discover that so many wonderful recipes could not be fit into one book. Thus we decided to limit the content to appetizers and desserts, a logical grouping for entertaining and, to some, the best parts of any meal.

We asked hundreds of Jewish groups for their best recipes — the most interesting, the most unusual, the most delicious, the most traditional. The response was heartwarming. Many groups that did not have cookbooks of their own wrote to offer encouragement. One hundred and twenty organizations had enough faith in us and the project to grant us permission to reprint their family treasures.

The best cooks in our community read thousands of recipes (on paper, they had to look good enough to eat). Those that passed this screening were then tested and re-tested in members' kitchens.

Once the selections were made, they were edited for accuracy and completeness. Where necessary, we clarified instructions or added some that would help a novice follow the recipe (after all, Grandma sometimes used a jelly glass instead of a measuring cup, and cutting an ingredient into "rather small pieces" just wouldn't hold up to universal interpretation). In some cases we added pan sizes and package sizes, and specified the number of servings or quantity made (though servings vary somewhat according to individual appetites and the rest of the menu). We also made certain that all recipes could be served by anyone observing Jewish dietary laws. Whenever feasible, original wording was retained.

After all the selected recipes were assembled, we couldn't resist adding a handful of our own personal favorites, which we have labeled "Editors' Choice."

The final result is a collection of those shining examples of our cooking that each of us likes to pull out when the occasion calls for our most outstanding recipe.

This has been a labor of love for committee members, testers, and everyone who tasted. The result has been worth the effort. We thank all of you who shared your recipes with us ... and proudly present THE CHOSEN: APPETIZERS & DESSERTS.

Marilyn Stone, Editor
April 15, 1982

*If your organization cookbook is not represented in this collection, we invite you to submit it for inclusion in future editions or cookbooks. Help us by marking the recipes you think are especially good. Send a copy of your book to Triad Publishing Co., P.O. Box 13096, Gainesville, Florida 32605.*

# Contents

# A word about appetizers
# ... and desserts

APPETIZERS

Whatever the occasion, it seems that food and entertaining go together. No food offers more flexibility than appetizers. They may be a prelude to dinner or the focus of your party food.

Finding good recipes doesn't seem to be as hard as choosing which ones to serve. If you are having a dinner party, you will want to select appetizers that are light, so as not to spoil your guests' appetites for the meal to follow. Two appetizers, perhaps one hot and one cold, should be enough. In place of appetizers, some people like to serve a first course in the living room. This is a nice touch that lets one dish do the work of two.

The all-appetizer party calls for a bit more planning. If you are having a cocktail party or open house, remember that some of your guests will want to eat lightly because they will be going to dinner afterward. Others will make the appetizers their entire meal.

We suggest that you offer variety. Try to balance dips and spreads with some pick-up foods. Texture and consistency are important, too. Some foods should be smooth and others crunchy. Give some thought to color, so that the same color doesn't appear dominant in every dish. Balance your old stand-by recipes with a few new ones. Make sure the same main ingredient, such as cheese, isn't repeated too often. Include both hot and cold dishes. Offer fresh vegetables for the dieters.

Think of yourself as well. Unless you want to spend the whole party in the kitchen, serve only one or two hors d'oeuvres that need to be heated at the last minute. Set out as much as possible on your buffet table in advance, and provide small plates for your guests so that they may help themselves and then move away from the table, leaving room for others.

DESSERTS

If you are planning a single dessert as the last course of a dinner party, the choices are numerous. We would caution you only to avoid repetition of those ingredients served in the main course. For example, do not serve apricot mousse in the same meal as duck with apricot sauce.

All-dessert parties need planning, just as all-appetizer parties. Variety is the key here, too, regarding color, texture, main ingredient, etc. We try always to include one chocolate dessert (for those who think dessert isn't dessert unless it's chocolate) and at least one dessert without chocolate or nuts for those who are allergic to them. If there are to be no plates or forks, serve only cookies or form cakes. A bowl of fresh fruit makes a nice edible centerpiece, or you may offer a bowl of fresh fruit salad as a low-calorie selection.

## OR BOTH

If you are planning a full-scale "come for appetizers, stay for dessert" party, omitting the in-between courses, the same pointers apply as for all-appetizer or all-dessert parties. The only other thing to consider is that since this party is taking the place of a meal, at least a few of the appetizers should be hearty and filling.

# appetizers

# Dips & spreads

## Appetizer Cheese Cake

KITCHEN KAPERS   ELMIRA CHAPTER OF HADASSAH   ELMIRA, NEW YORK

2 cups sour cream
½ cup finely chopped
 green pepper
½ cup finely chopped
 celery
¼ cup minced onion
2 teaspoons lemon juice
1 teaspoon Worcestershire
 sauce
⅛ teaspoon paprika
6 drops Tabasco sauce
6 ounces blue cheese,
 crumbled
1 cup cheese-flavored
 cracker crumbs

In a medium bowl, combine sour cream, green pepper, celery, onion, lemon juice, Worcestershire sauce, paprika, and Tabasco. Remove one cup of the mixture and mix it with the blue cheese. Put the rest in a 6-cup serving dish and smooth the surface. Spoon on ½ cup of the cracker crumbs and then the sour cream-blue cheese mixture. Cover with remaining crumbs. Refrigerate.

Serves 12 to 14.

*Spread on crackers or cocktail rye.*

# Bleu Cheese Log

THE MELTING POT   JEWISH COMMUNITY CENTER   AMHERST, MASSACHUSETTS

4 ounces bleu cheese
8 ounces cream cheese
¼ cup butter or margarine
⅓ to ½ cup black olives,
  chopped
½ cup chopped nuts

Let all ingredients stand at room temperature for 1 hour. Mash the cheeses and butter together. Mix in the olives and about ⅓ of the nuts. Form into a log and roll in nuts. Refrigerate.

Remove from refrigerator 1 hour before serving.


# Best-Ever Roquefort Dip

PORTAL TO GOOD COOKING   WOMEN'S AMERICAN ORT, VIII   CHICAGO, ILLINOIS

2 cups thick sour cream
⅛ teaspoon garlic salt
6 drops Worcestershire
  sauce
3 ounces Roquefort cheese

Combine sour cream, garlic salt, and Worcestershire; blend thoroughly. Rub cheese against side of bowl to break up, but do not mash. Add to sour cream and mix with fork.

Serve with potato chips, carrot or celery sticks, etc.

Makes 2½ cups.

* Also makes a good salad dressing.


# Camembert or Brie with Nut Butter

IN GOOD TASTE   JEWISH COMMUNITY CENTER OF STATEN ISLAND   STATEN ISLAND, NEW YORK

8-ounce cheese wheel,
  chilled
¼ cup butter, softened
⅓ cup coarsely ground
  pecans
2 tablespoons lemon juice
Few drops Tabasco sauce

Cream butter until soft and fluffy. Add pecans, lemon juice, and Tabasco and mix thoroughly.

Slice cheese in half horizontally, as for a sandwich.

Spread nut butter on each inside surface of the cheese, then reassemble into its original form.

Serve with unsalted crackers.

Makes about 1½ cups.

# Curry-Cheese Ball

EDITOR'S CHOICE

8 ounces yellow cheese,
  grated
3 ounces cream cheese
2 cloves garlic, mashed
½ cup chopped nuts
  (pecans or walnuts)
Curry powder

Mix cheeses, garlic, and nuts. Form into a ball and roll in curry powder. Chill.

Freezes very well. Leftovers can be remolded into a smaller ball and frozen. After defrosting, roll in curry powder again, and it will look like you just made it.

*This can be made with a wide variety of cheeses and proportions. Use the recipe only as a guide. Medium sharp cheddar (in place of yellow cheese) and pecans are an especially good combination.*

# Cheddar-Chutney Spread

WHAT'S COOKING AT SHIR AMI   CONGREGATION SHIR AMI   CASTRO VALLEY, CALIFORNIA

1 pound aged sharp
  Cheddar cheese, diced
½ cup Trader Vic's
  Chutney
3 tablespoons curry
  powder
1 teaspoon powdered
  ginger

Combine all the ingredients in a blender jar or food processor. Blend well and pack in 4- or 5-ounce petits pots. Store in refrigerator.

*The flavor will be different, but other chutneys may be substituted with equally good results.*

# Cheese Ball

WHAT'S COOKING AT SHIR AMI   CONGREGATION SHIR AMI   CASTRO VALLEY, CALIFORNIA

16 ounces cream cheese
8 ounces sharp Cheddar
  cheese, shredded
1 tablespoon chopped
  pimiento
1 tablespoon chopped green
  pepper
1 teaspoon chopped onion
2 teaspoons Worcestershire
  sauce
Dash *each* salt, pepper,
  paprika
Chopped nuts

Have ingredients at room temperature. Combine all ingredients except the nuts. Roll into a ball. Wrap in waxed paper and refrigerate 24 hours. Roll in nuts before serving.

The cheese ball may be made ahead and frozen.

# Beer Dip

IN THE BEGINNING   KEBEL KODESH BENE ISRAEL   CINCINNATI, OHIO

1 cup beer
1 pound sharp Cheddar
  cheese, shredded
1¼ ounces Roquefort
  cheese, crumbled
2 tablespoons butter
½ medium onion, chopped
2 cloves garlic, minced *or*
  1 teaspoon garlic powder
1 teaspoon Worcestershire
½ teaspoon Tabasco

Heat beer and cool. Soften both cheeses and butter; cream together in mixer. Add the onion, garlic, Worcestershire, and Tabasco. Add beer to thin to spreading consistency.

Makes about 3 cups.

# Beer Cheese Ball

EDITOR'S CHOICE

1 pound Cheddar cheese
1 pound Swiss cheese
1 teaspoon dry mustard
1 small clove garlic,
  minced
1 teaspoon Worcestershire
  sauce
1 cup beer
1 cup nuts or parsley,
  chopped

Shred cheeses. Add mustard, garlic, and Worcestershire. Mix. Gradually add beer while beating with mixer or food processor. Chill about 1 hour. Then form into a ball and roll in chopped nuts or parsley.

Makes one 6-inch cheese ball.

# Baked Cheese Loaf

INSPIRATIONS FROM RENA HADASSAH   RENA HADASSAH   MT. VERNON, NEW YORK

Farmer cheese brick
Garlic salt
Paprika
½ cup chopped chives

Place cheese in ovenproof glass dish and sprinkle with garlic salt, paprika, and chives. Bake in a 350° oven for about 20 minutes. or till the brick "sags" as it starts to melt. Serve warm.

*The baked cheese has a smooth texture and is very nice with crackers.*

# Herbed Cheese (A Boursin Substitute)

FROM SOUP TO NOSH   NORTHERN VIRGINIA HADASSAH   FALLS CHURCH, VIRGINIA

8 ounces cream cheese
½ teaspoon lemon juice
1 tablespoon oregano
⅛ teaspoon cayenne
¼ teaspoon black pepper,
   freshly ground
2 tablespoons butter
1 garlic clove, mashed
2 tablespoons parsley, very
   finely chopped
½ teaspoon salt

Blend all ingredients together and allow to sit before serving. Freezes very well.

   Makes about 1 cup.

* *Better than the real thing!*

# Sage-Derby Cheese

FOOD FOR THOUGHT COOKBOOK   TEMPLE EMUNAH SISTERHOOD   LEXINGTON, MASSACHUSETTS

8 ounces cream cheese,
  room temperature
2 tablespoons chopped
  green onion *or* 1
  tablespoon dried minced
  green onion
2 tablespoons sage
2 tablespoons poppy seed

Beat together cream cheese, sage, and green onion. Cover tightly and refrigerate until firm. Shape into flattened balls. Lightly press sides and top with poppy seed. Chill and serve with crackers.

Makes about 1 cup.

*\* Can be shaped into one ball and coated with seeds.*

# Mock Chopped Herring

TRY IT — YOU'LL LIKE IT   JACKSONVILLE JEWISH CENTER SISTERHOOD   JACKSONVILLE, FLORIDA

1 can sardines, mashed
1 onion, chopped
1 apple, chopped
1 slice white bread, soaked
  in vinegar
Pinch salt
1 tablespoon mayonnaise
2 hard-boiled eggs

Chop all the ingredients together until very fine. It will make a thick spread. Serve with party rye or crackers.

Serves 12 to 14.

# Cheese and Sardine Mold

FAIRMOUNT TEMPLE COOKBOOK  FAIRMOUNT TEMPLE SISTERHOOD  CLEVELAND, OHIO

6 tins sardines, skinless
  and boneless
½ cup butter or oil from
  sardines
8-ounce package cream
  cheese (plain or with
  pimiento)
8-ounce package relish
  cheese
Horseradish (white or beet)
  to taste
Parsley

Drain sardines, reserving the oil.

Combine all ingredients and beat with electric mixer. Mold into the shape of a pineapple, using parsley for the leaves (or you can use the top of a real pineapple).

Makes 5½ cups.


# Gefilte Fish Dip

FAVORITE RECIPES  WOMEN OF BRIT SHALOM CONGREGATION  STATE COLLEGE, PENNSYLVANIA

1 jar (1 lb.) gefilte fish
8 ounces cream cheese
2 tablespoons prepared
  horseradish
1 teaspoon lemon juice
½ teaspoon salt
Dash pepper

Drain fish, reserving 3 tablespoons of the broth. Mash the fish. Add rest of ingredients, including the reserved fish broth. Blend well.

Chill in refrigerator for at least 1 hour.

Makes 3 cups.


# Caviar Pie

POT OF GOLD  SISTERHOOD, CONGREGATION HAR SHALOM  POTOMAC, MARYLAND

6 hard-cooked eggs,
  chopped
1½ tablespoons mayonnaise
3 or 4 scallions, with green
  tops, thinly sliced
Dash black pepper
1 jar black caviar (4 oz.)
1 pint sour cream

Combine eggs, mayonnaise, scallions, and pepper. Spread evenly on the bottom of an 8- or 9-inch pie plate. Spread caviar over egg mixture; cover caviar with sour cream. Refrigerate several hours, until firm.

Serve (with a butter spreader) with party pumpernickel, rye bread, or crackers.

Serves 6 to 10.

* May substitute 2 medium onions, chopped, for the egg layer.

# Liptauer Spread

COUNCIL'S COOK-IN  NATIONAL COUNCIL OF JEWISH WOMEN  BAYSHORE, NEW JERSEY

2 anchovy fillets
1 slice onion
8 ounces cream cheese, softened
3 tablespoons thick sour cream
1 tablespoon prepared mustard
1½ teaspoons caraway seeds
1 teaspoon capers
½ teaspoon salt
Parsley sprigs, anchovy fillets, paprika (optional)

Finely chop the anchovy fillets and onion. Beat the cream cheese and sour cream together until well blended. Add to anchovy and onion and mix well. Add mustard, caraway seeds, capers, and salt. Beat until smooth.

Transfer to a serving dish and shape into a smooth mound. Refrigerate. Garnish with parsley sprigs, anchovy fillets, paprika, or all.

Makes about 1¾ cups.

# Hungarian Cheese Dip

FAVORITE RECIPES  CONGREGATION KOL EMETH  PALO ALTO, CALIFORNIA

16 ounces cream cheese
1 cup butter or margarine, softened
½ cup sour cream
¼ cup sherry
2½ teaspoons paprika
4 anchovies, mashed
¼ cup chopped green onion
1½ teaspoons caraway seed
¾ teaspoon dry mustard
1 teaspoon salt
½ teaspoon coarse pepper

Beat cream cheese and butter till smooth and well blended. Beat in rest of ingredients. Cover and refrigerate overnight.

Serve with party rye bread or rye crackers.

Makes 3½ cups.

# Maida Heatter's Family Secret

FROM DORA WITH LOVE  SISTERHOOD OF GARDEN CITY JEWISH CENTER  GARDEN CITY, NEW YORK

16 ounces cream cheese
¼ cup butter
1½ tablespoons finely cut shallots
1½ tablespoons chopped capers
1 teaspoon paprika
Pinch cayenne
1 teaspoon anchovy paste
2 or 3 anchovy fillets, coarsely chopped

Cream the cheese and butter. Add all other ingredients and mix well. The last 6 items may be increased or adjusted to taste. Pack in a crock. Let it ripen for a day or two. It improves! Serve with homemade Melba Toast.

Makes about 2 cups.

# Salmon Party Ball

FLAVORED WITH LOVE  ADAT ARI EL SISTERHOOD  NORTH HOLLYWOOD, CALIFORNIA

1 can (1 lb.) salmon
8 ounces cream cheese, softened
1 tablespoon lemon juice
2 teaspoons grated onion
1 teaspoon prepared horseradish
¼ teaspoon salt
¼ teaspoon liquid smoke, optional
½ cup chopped pecans
3 tablespoons snipped parsley

Drain and flake salmon, removing skin and bones. Combine salmon, cream cheese, lemon juice, onion, horseradish, salt, and liquid smoke. Mix thoroughly. Chill overnight.

Combine pecans and parsley. Shape salmon mixture into a ball. Roll in nut mixture. Chill well.

Serve with assorted crackers.

# Cuban Tuna

POT OF GOLD  SISTERHOOD, CONGREGATION HAR SHALOM  POTOMAC, MARYLAND

1 can (6½ oz.) tuna, drained
2 tablespoons mayonnaise
1 cup small curd cottage cheese or 8 ounces cream cheese, softened

Combine all ingredients and mix together until smooth, preferably with electric beater. Refrigerate.

Makes 2 cups.

*Very light and fresh-tasting. Can be used as a spread or a salad.*

# Tuna Pâté

EAT IN GOOD HEALTH   CONGREGATION B'NAI ISRAEL   ROCKVILLE, CONNECTICUT

8 ounces cream cheese,
  softened
2 tablespoons chopped
  parsley
1 teaspoon dried instant
  onion
2 cans (7½ oz. *each*) tuna,
  drained and flaked
2 tablespoons chili sauce
½ teaspoon hot pepper
  sauce

Combine cream cheese, parsley, onion, tuna, chili sauce, and pepper sauce. Add extra chili sauce or pepper sauce as desired. Mix well. Chill 3 hours. Serve with crackers.

Makes about 3 cups.

# Rozie's Party Spread

SUPER CHEF   BETH ISRAEL SISTERHOOD   WARREN, OHIO

1 cup "salad" green olives
  (these come as broken
  pieces; if too large, cut
  up)
8 ounces cream cheese,
  softened
½ cup mayonnaise
½ cup (heaping) chopped
  pecans
Dash pepper
Dash garlic powder

Drain olives, reserving 2 tablespoons juice. Combine cream cheese and reserved olive juice and mix until smooth. Add all other ingredients and combine thoroughly. Refrigerate, tightly covered, for 24 to 48 hours for flavors to blend.

Serve with crackers. Will keep well if tightly covered.

Makes about 2½ cups.

*Also great as a stuffing for celery.*

# Broccoli Cheese Dip

WHAT'S COOKING IN BIRMINGHAM   B'NAI B'RITH WOMEN   BIRMINGHAM, ALABAMA

1 can cream of mushroom
  soup (undiluted)
1 can (2 oz.) mushroom
  pieces, drained
1 small garlic cheese roll
1 medium onion, finely
  diced
½ cup butter or margarine
1 package (10 oz.) frozen
  chopped broccoli

Heat together soup, mushrooms, and cheese. Sauté the onion in the butter; add to mixture. Cook broccoli and drain well. Add.

Serve in a chafing dish with crackers, corn chips, or raw vegetables.

* *We successfully substituted ½ pound medium cheddar cheese and 2 cloves garlic, crushed, for the cheese roll.*

# Cheese and Mushroom Ball
TRY IT, YOU'LL LIKE IT   TEMPLE BETH EL SISTERHOOD   RICHMOND, VIRGINIA

1 can (4 oz.) mushroom
  stems and pieces
8 ounces cream cheese,
  softened
1 tablespoon finely minced
  onion
½ teaspoon salt
1 teaspoon Worcestershire
  sauce

Drain mushrooms and finely chop. Mix into cream cheese with onion, salt, and Worcestershire sauce. Chill thoroughly so mixture will be easy to handle. Shape into a ball.

# Hummos Bi Tahini
RECIPES FROM WOMEN OF BRIT SHALOM   JEWISH COMMUNITY CENTER   STATE COLLEGE, PENNSYLVANIA

1 can chick-peas
1 clove garlic, minced
Juice of 1 large lemon
½ teaspoon salt
½ teaspoon pepper,
  cracked
3 tablespoons sesame
  Tahini
2 tablespoons chopped
  parsley

Drain chick-peas; reserve liquid.

In blender, place chick-peas, ¼ cup liquid from can, garlic, lemon juice, salt, and pepper. Blend to paste.

Remove to bowl and mix in well the sesame Tahini. Chill.

Garnish with parsley and serve with crisp crackers or Arabian flat bread to dip.

Makes about 2 cups.

*This can also be made in a food processor.*

# Artichoke Spread

THE STUFFED BAGEL  HADASSAH CHAPTER  COLUMBIA, SOUTH CAROLINA

2 cans artichoke hearts,
  drained
1 cup Parmesan cheese
1 cup mayonnaise
1¾ teaspoons garlic salt

Pick apart artichoke hearts until all the leaves are separated. Mix mayonnaise and cheese and add to artichokes. Add salt; sprinkle some extra Parmesan cheese on top.

Bake in a 350° oven for about 20 minutes until hot. Serve on crackers.

Makes about 3 or 4 cups. Will serve 10.

*Try unbaked as a spread. Can also be used as a vegetable.*

# Spinach Spread

NIBBLES, NOSHES, AND GOURMET DELIGHTS  TEMPLE IN THE PINES  HOLLYWOOD, FLORIDA

2 packages frozen chopped
  spinach, drained
1 package vegetable soup
  mix (dry)
1¼ pints sour cream
½ bunch scallions,
  chopped
1 can water chestnuts,
  sliced and chopped
Lowry's seasoned salt, to
  taste

Mix all ingredients well. (Can be molded with hands.) Serve with pumpernickel bread.

Makes about 2½ cups.

# Red Bean Dip

FROM CHARLESTON WITH LOVE  SYNAGOGUE EMANU-EL SISTERHOOD  CHARLESTON, SOUTH CAROLINA

1 can (15 oz.) red beans
½ cup onion, chopped
1 large piece garlic
¼ teaspoon salt
¼ teaspoon cumin
Dash Tabasco sauce

Drain beans, reserving ¼ cup liquid. Combine the bean liquid with all the ingredients and mix in a blender. Let sit for several hours.

Heat and serve with corn chips.

Makes about 2 cups.

# Olivacado Dip

IN THE BEGINNING KEBEL KODESH BENE ISRAEL CINCINNATI, OHIO

1 ripe avocado
1 can (2½ oz.) sliced or chopped black olives, drained well
1 tablespoon grated onion
½ teaspoon seasoned salt
Juice of ½ lemon or lime

Cut avocado in half lengthwise. Carefully remove avocado flesh with a spoon. Save the shells.

Combine avocado, olives, onion, seasoned salt, and lemon juice. Mix thoroughly. Heap into avocado shells.

Serve with crisp slices of carrot, turnip, radish, kohlrabi, or other fresh vegetables (worth trying unusual ones).

Fills 2 avocado shells.

# Guacamole

EDITOR'S CHOICE

1 large, fully ripe avocado (10 to 12 oz.)
1 small tomato, juiced and chopped
1 to 2 tablespoons finely chopped onion or green onion
1 teaspoon minced fresh coriander (Chinese parsley or cilantro) or ¼ teaspoon ground dry coriander
1 to 2 teaspoons minced canned California green chile (seeds and pith removed)
¼ teaspoon minced, canned, small hot chile (such as jalepeno) or a few drops liquid hot pepper seasoning
1 clove garlic, mashed
Salt to taste (about ¼ t.)

Peel and pit avocado and mash coarsely with a fork. Mix in tomato and onion to taste, coriander, green chile, hot chile (or liquid pepper to taste), and salt to season.

Serve at room temperature or chilled; cover to refrigerate up to 3 days. (To freeze, do not add onion until mixture is thawed for serving.)

Serve with corn chips.

Makes about 1 cup guacamole.

* For special occasions, place a layer of corn chips on an ovenproof serving platter; sprinkle with ½ cup shredded Monterey Jack or other mild yellow cheese, then a small amount of sharper Cheddar (for added color). Place in a 300° oven for 3 to 5 minutes to melt the cheese. Serve with the guacamole spooned into a lettuce leaf placed over the top of the corn chips.

# Chile Con Queso Dip

WHAT'S COOKING? HADASSAH CHAPTER LOS ALAMOS, NEW MEXICO

2 pounds mild cheese
1 large onion, diced fine
Butter
1 can tomatoes with green chile

Melt the cheese in a double boiler. Brown onion in the butter and add to the melted cheese. Add the tomatoes and mix well. Serve hot with corn chips or raw vegetables.

Makes about 4 cups.

*Also good as it cools down.*


# Daffodil Dip

SPECIALTIES OF THE HOUSE TEMPLE EMANUEL DAVENPORT, IOWA

8 ounces cream cheese, softened
½ cup mayonnaise
1 hard-cooked egg
½ cup chopped parsley
2 tablespoons chopped onion
1 garlic clove, minced
1 tablespoon anchovy paste
Dash pepper

Combine cream cheese and mayonnaise. Chop egg white and add with parsley, onion, garlic, anchovy paste, and pepper. Mix thoroughly. Sprinkle chopped egg yolk over the top.

Serve with fresh vegetables.

Makes 2½ cups.


# Crispy Cauliflower Dip

MENU MAGIC BETH ISRAEL SISTERHOOD FLINT, MICHIGAN

1 head cauliflower
2 hard-cooked eggs
1 small onion
2 cups mayonnaise

Wash the cauliflower and tear into small flowerets. Place over ice cubes and refrigerate.

Grate eggs and onion. Add mayonnaise. Mix well.

To serve, put dip mixture into a small bowl. Put toothpicks in the small pieces of cauliflower so that they can be dipped.

Serves 15 to 20.

*Dip may be used with other raw vegetables – carrots, celery, etc.*

# Herb Dip for Raw Vegetables

SISTERHOOD COOKERY   SISTERHOOD OF BROOKLYN HEIGHTS SYNAGOGUE   BROOKLYN, NEW YORK

1 cup mayonnaise
½ cup sour cream
¼ teaspoon marjoram,
   crushed
¼ teaspoon basil, crushed
¼ teaspoon savory,
   crushed
¼ teaspoon thyme, crushed
¼ teaspoon salt
½ teaspoon Worcestershire
⅛ teaspoon curry
1 tablespoon minced onion
1½ teaspoons lemon juice
1 teaspoon chopped parsley

Combine all ingredients. Mix thoroughly and chill.

Serve with raw vegetables such as celery, carrots, cauliflower, green pepper, cherry tomatoes, and cucumber slices.

Makes 1½ cups.

# Curry Dip for Fresh Vegetables

THE FORT SHERIDAN & GREAT LAKES JEWISH CHAPEL COOKBOOK   GREAT LAKES NTC   GREAT LAKES, ILLINOIS

1 tablespoon sugar
1 teaspoon garlic salt
1 teaspoon curry powder
1 teaspoon horseradish
1 teaspoon grated onion
1 teaspoon cider vinegar
½ cup sour cream
½ cup mayonnaise

Combine ingredients and mix well. Chill several hours before serving.

Makes 1 cup.

# Cold appetizers

## Marinated Mushrooms and Artichoke Hearts

THE HAPPY COOKER OF TEMPLE SHALOM   TEMPLE SHALOM   WEST NEWTON, MASSACHUSETTS

2 packages (9 oz. *each*)
  frozen artichoke hearts
2 pounds small fresh
  mushrooms
1½ cups water
1 cup cider vinegar
½ cup salad oil
1 clove garlic, halved
1½ tablespoons salt
½ teaspoon black pepper,
  freshly ground
½ teaspoon thyme
½ teaspoon oregano
½ teaspoon chervil
1 bay leaf
Chopped parsley

Cook artichoke hearts according to package directions until barely tender, being careful not to overcook. Drain. Slice mushrooms in half through stems; combine with artichoke hearts.

In large bowl, combine water, vinegar, oil, garlic, salt, pepper, and herbs; add artichokes and mushrooms. Toss lightly. Marinate overnight.

Serves 16.

# Mushrooms à la Greque I

THE PREPARED TABLE   SOLOMON SCHECHTER DAY SCHOOL   BALA CYNWYD, PENNSYLVANIA

1½ pounds small white
  mushrooms
1 cup water
1 cup olive oil
Juice of 3 lemons
1 tablespoon white vinegar
1 rib celery, chopped
1 rib fennel, chopped, or a
  few fennel seeds, crushed
1 clove garlic
½ teaspoon thyme
½ bay leaf
¾ teaspoon ground
  coriander
8 peppercorns
¼ teaspoon salt

Combine all ingredients in a saucepan. Bring to a boil, then simmer for 5 minutes, stirring occasionally. Pour into a bowl and refrigerate overnight.

Serve with toothpicks or on a garnished plate. This keeps a long time in the refrigerator. (Oil may cloud, but clears when warmed to room temperature.)

Serves about 8.

*\* Enjoy the Middle Eastern taste with American ease.*

# Mushrooms à la Greque II

SALT AND PEPPER TO TASTE   SISTERHOOD CONGREGATION ANSHEI ISRAEL   TUCSON, ARIZONA

1 pound fresh mushrooms
½ cup olive oil or
  vegetable oil, or
  combination
½ cup water
¼ cup dry white wine
2 tablespoons minced
  onion
2 tablespoons lemon juice
1 tablespoon tomato paste
1 bay leaf
Salt and pepper to taste

Rinse mushrooms and drain. If large, cut into bite-size pieces. Place remaining ingredients in a saucepan and bring to a boil. Lower heat and simmer 5 minutes. Add mushrooms. Simmer 8 to 10 minutes, stirring occasionally.

Remove mushrooms with slotted spoon. Continue cooking liquid a few minutes to reduce volume. Pour over mushrooms.

Chill and serve cold with toothpicks.

Serves about 6.

# Marinated Raw Mushrooms

KITCHEN MAGIC  SISTERHOOD OF BET TORAH  MT. KISCO, NEW YORK

½ pound small mushrooms
1 large onion, diced
½ cup olive oil
3 tablespoons wine vinegar
½ teaspoon dried oregano, crushed
¼ teaspoon salt
Black pepper, to taste

Remove stems from mushrooms. Mix all other ingredients together. Add mushroom caps and toss until coated. Let stand at room temperature for several hours or refrigerate for at least 5 hours.

Serve with toothpicks.


# Dill Marinated Brussels Sprouts

THE COOKERY  TEMPLE BETH EL  SOUTH BEND, INDIANA

2 packages (10 oz. each) frozen brussels sprouts
¼ cup salad oil
2 tablespoons lemon juice
2 tablespoons finely chopped onion
1 clove garlic, minced
1 teaspoon chopped fresh dill (or ½ teaspoon dried dill)
Salt and pepper to taste

Cook sprouts until crisp-tender. Drain and rinse in cold water. Combine rest of ingredients in a bowl, add brussels sprouts, and mix lightly. Cover and chill overnight, stirring occasionally. Serve chilled.

Serves 6.


# Dilled Zucchini

ARTISTRY IN THE KITCHEN  TEMPLE WOMEN'S ASSOCIATION  CLEVELAND, OHIO

1½ pounds zucchini, small and tender
1 cup white vinegar
2 cups water
⅔ cup sugar
½ teaspoon salt
Flower heads of ½ bunch dill
Juice of 2 lemons
1 pint sour cream
1 Bermuda onion, sliced

Scrub zucchini, cut off ends, and slice in ⅛-inch rounds. Bring to a boil the vinegar, water, sugar, salt, and dill. Add zucchini and simmer for 10 minutes. Let cool in liquor. Then remove dill and discard. Drain zucchini well, reserving the liquid. Chill.

Over the chilled zucchini, pour lemon juice, sour cream, and onion. Combine with the reserved liquor, adding more sugar if desired. Refrigerate.

# Marinated Vegetables

EDITORS' CHOICE

½ head cauliflower, cut in
  large flowerets and sliced
2 carrots, pared, cut in
  thin strips, 2 inches long
2 stalks celery, cut in
  1-inch pieces (1 cup)
1 green pepper, cut in
  2-inch strips
1 jar (4 oz.) pimento,
  drained, cut in strips
1 jar (3 oz.) pitted green
  olives
¾ cup wine vinegar,
  preferably white
½ cup olive or salad oil
2 tablespoons sugar
½ teaspoon oregano
1 teaspoon salt
¼ teaspoon pepper
¼ cup water

Combine all ingredients and bring to a boil. Simmer 5 minutes. Cool and refrigerate at least 24 hours. Drain well.

Serves 6.

# Eggplant Caviar

LIKE MAMA USED TO MAKE   ANN ARBOR CHAPTER OF HADASSAH   ANN ARBOR, MICHIGAN

1 small eggplant (unpeeled)
1 onion
1 green pepper
1 can (4 oz.) mushrooms
Garlic to taste
⅓ cup salad oil
1 can (6 oz.) tomato paste
¼ cup water
2 tablespoons wine vinegar
½ cup chopped stuffed
  olives
3 tablespoons pine nuts
1½ teaspoons sugar
½ teaspoon oregano
Salt and pepper to taste

Chop finely the eggplant, onion, green pepper, mushrooms, and garlic. Place in a pot with the oil and simmer for 10 minutes.

Stir the remaining ingredients into the pot. Cover and simmer for 30 minutes. Chill and serve cold. May be frozen.

Makes about 3 cups.

# Eggplant Appetizer I

THE COOK'S BOOK  SUBURBAN JEWISH COMMUNITY CENTER  HAVERTOWN, PENNSYLVANIA

1 medium eggplant
4 to 5 tablespoons oil
3 large cloves garlic,
  mashed
1 teaspoon salt (or to taste)
1 medium onion, grated or
  finely chopped
Olives, green pepper,
  and/or green tomatoes for
  garnish

Put eggplant under low flame in broiler; when top is soft, turn to cook other side. When eggplant is completely soft, remove from broiler. Scoop pulp out onto a board or colander and let drain 10 minutes.

In a bowl, mix oil into pulp and let cool. Then mix in garlic, onion, and salt. Refrigerate.

Serve with vegetable garnish and crackers, cocktail rye, or pumpernickel.

Makes about 1½ cups.

# Eggplant Appetizer II

TRY IT, YOU'LL LIKE IT  JACKSONVILLE JEWISH CENTER SISTERHOOD  JACKSONVILLE, FLORIDA

1 large eggplant
1 medium bell pepper
1 very small onion, minced
1 tablespoon oil
Salt to taste

Bake eggplant at 350° for 45 minutes. Remove from oven and place on a slanted board in sink, bulb side down, and slash several times to allow the juice to drain out. Peel.

Broil the bell pepper, turning several times until it is black. Run cold water over it quickly, and pinch off all the black. Remove seeds and stem.

Put broiled pepper and peeled eggplant into a wooden chopping bowl with the minced onion. Chop until smooth. Add oil and salt and continue chopping. Chill.

Makes 1½ to 2 cups.

*Garnish with chopped tomato and serve with party rye.*

# Vegetable Chopped Liver I

LIKE MAMMA USED TO MAKE   ANN ARBOR CHAPTER OF HADASSAH   ANN ARBOR, MICHIGAN

1 pound fresh string beans
4 or 5 medium onions, diced
¼ cup butter or chicken fat
4 hard-boiled eggs
10 walnuts
Salt and pepper to taste

Cook string beans and drain well. Sauté onions in fat. Mix all ingredients together and chop. Season to taste. Chill and serve as an appetizer.

# Vegetable Chopped Liver II

EDITORS' CHOICE

1 can (16 oz.) string beans, drained
3 large onions
2 or 3 tablespoons oil
8 or 9 eggs, hard-boiled

Chop onions and sauté in oil until they are very dark brown, but not burned. Drain off oil and add onions to string beans. Chop together with the eggs. Add some of the oil for a smoother mixture.

Mound in a bowl and serve with cocktail rye or crackers.

# Pareve Chopped Liver

NUI WHAT'S COOKING   THE WOMEN'S LEAGUE OF THE YESHIVA   SPRING VALLEY, NEW YORK

1 medium onion, chopped
1 medium can French cut string beans, drained
2 hard-cooked eggs
6 walnuts
2 tablespoons creamy peanut butter
Salt and pepper to taste

Mix together the onion, string beans, eggs, and walnuts, and chop until very fine. Add the peanut butter, salt, and pepper. Mix well.

Makes about 2 cups.

*Chopped onion may be sautéed in a small amount of oil.*

# Dairy Liver

FROM GENERATION TO GENERATION  B'NAI AMOONA SISTERHOOD  ST. LOUIS, MISSOURI

1½ pounds mushrooms,
  sliced
½ cup diced onion
3 tablespoons salad oil
1 hard-cooked egg
½ teaspoon salt
¼ teaspoon pepper

Cook mushrooms and onions in oil for 10 minutes, stirring occasionally. Drain well. Chop mushrooms, onions, and egg with knife until smooth. Add salt and pepper. Chill.

Serve as an appetizer on lettuce leaves or as a spread.

Makes about 2 cups.

# Cheese Biscuits with Dates

HISTORICALLY SPEAKING  KAHAL KADOSH BETH ELOHIM  CHARLESTON, SOUTH CAROLINA

½ cup butter
¾ pound grated sharp
  cheddar cheese (N.Y.
  State)
1 package (7½-8 oz.) dates
  (pitted)
2 cups flour
Confectioners' sugar

Cream butter and cheese. Mix in flour. Roll thin. Cut into circles with biscuit cutter. Fold around whole dates.

Bake in a 350° oven until very brown. Sprinkle with confectioners' sugar when slightly cool.

* This is an unusual combination that is delicious.

# Egg Salad Cups

THE NEW PORTAL TO GOOD COOKING, VOL. II  WOMEN'S AMERICAN ORT, VIII  CHICAGO, ILLINOIS

12 thin slices bread
Butter, softened
5 hard-cooked eggs, grated
¼ cup minced green
  pepper
1 teaspoon grated onion
¼ cup mayonnaise
1 tablespoon vinegar
1 tablespoon Worcestershire
  sauce
Drop Tabasco sauce
½ teaspoon salt
½ teaspoon dry mustard
Dash cayenne pepper
Parsley, pimento, or
  stuffed olives for garnish

Cut bread into 2-inch rounds. Spread both sides lightly with butter. Press into small muffin cups.

Bake in a 375° oven until edges are lightly browned (about 8 to 10 minutes).

Meanwhile, mix the remaining ingredients together. Fill toasted bread cups. Garnish with bits of parsley, pimento, or sliced stuffed olives.

Makes 1 dozen.

*May eliminate bread cups and serve egg salad with melba toast or crackers. It also makes a nice mold with red caviar on the top.

# Egg Salad Mold

PORTFOLIO OF COOKERY   WOMEN'S AMERICAN ORT   BEVERLY HILLS, CALIFORNIA

1 package unflavored
  gelatin
½ cup cold water
2 tablespoons lemon juice
¼ teaspoon Worcestershire
  sauce
1 teaspoon salt
⅛ teaspoon cayenne pepper
4 hard-cooked eggs,
  mashed or chopped
¾ cup mayonnaise
½ cup chopped celery
½ cup chopped green
  pepper
¼ cup chopped pimiento
½ teaspoon grated onion

Soften gelatin in cold water. Combine with lemon juice, Worcestershire sauce, salt, and pepper in top of a double boiler and heat until gelatin is dissolved.

Combine with remaining ingredients and place in a 4-cup mold. Refrigerate.

* *Omit onion if you plan to keep overnight.*

# Salmon Mousse

ESSEN 'N FRESSEN   CONGREGATION BETH CHAIM   EAST WINDSOR, NEW JERSEY

1 envelope unflavored
  gelatin
2 teaspoons lemon juice
½ cup boiling water
1 medium onion, chopped
1 can (7¾ oz.) salmon,
  well-boned
1 cup mayonnaise
½ cup sour cream
1 heaping teaspoon dill
  weed
½ teaspoon paprika

Soften gelatin in lemon juice; dissolve in boiling water. Place in blender for ½ minute. Add onion; run blender for another ½ minute. Add salmon, mayonnaise, sour cream, dill, and paprika. Place in greased mold (a fish mold is perfect and beautiful, too). Chill several hours or overnight.

Serve with cucumber slices or rye bread. Delicious and easy!

Makes 3 cups.

* *Can also be made in food processor. Adjust times accordingly.*

# Salmon Mousse Canape

EAT IN GOOD HEALTH   CONGREGATION B'NAI ISRAEL   ROCKVILLE, CONNECTICUT

1 can (16 oz.) salmon
1 envelope unflavored
  gelatin
½ cup boiling water
½ cup mayonnaise
1 tablespoon lemon juice
1 tablespoon chopped
  capers
1 tablespoon parsley
1 small onion, chopped
½ teaspoon Tabasco sauce
¼ teaspoon paprika

Drain salmon, reserving ¼ cup juice.

Combine salmon juice and gelatin in blender. When gelatin is dissolved, add boiling water; blend. Add all other ingredients and mix thoroughly.

Pour into an oiled 1½-quart mold. Chill until firm.

Serve with crackers.

Serves 10 to 12.

# Caviar Mousse

THE WONDERFUL WORLD OF COOKING   BALDWIN HADASSAH   BALDWIN, NEW YORK

1 jar (4 oz.) red caviar
1 envelope unflavored
  gelatin
¼ cup cold water
2 tablespoons grated onion
1 tablespoon lemon juice
½ teaspoon salt
1 cup dairy sour cream
1 cup heavy cream,
  whipped

Set aside 1 tablespoon caviar for garnish. Press remaining caviar through a fine sieve with the back of a large spoon.

Soften gelatin in cold water in a small saucepan for 5 minutes. Dissolve over low heat. Cool slightly.

Combine sieved caviar, onion, lemon juice, salt, and sour cream in a medium size bowl; blend well. Stir in the gelatin. Fold in whipped cream. Turn mixture into an oiled 4-cup mold. Chill until firm.

To serve, unmold onto chilled plate. Garnish with reserved caviar. Serve with melba toast.

Makes about 4 cups.

# Caviar Mold

KITCHEN MAGIC  SISTERHOOD OF BET TORAH  MT. KISCO, NEW YORK

1 onion
6 hard-boiled eggs
1 package unflavored
  kosher gelatin
2 tablespoons lemon juice
2 tablespoons cold water
4 ounces caviar
1 cup mayonnaise
1 teaspoon Worcestershire
  sauce
Salt and pepper to taste

Grate onion; sieve the eggs.

Dilute gelatin in lemon juice and water. Dissolve in double boiler over hot water. Add to other ingredients. Pour into a 6-inch mold, greased with salad oil or olive oil. Chill for several hours. Unmold and serve with crackers.

Makes about 3 cups.


# Tuna Mousse

FAVORITE RECIPES  CONGREGATION BETHAYNU SISTERHOOD  BEACHWOOD, OHIO

1 envelope unflavored
  gelatin
2 tablespoons lemon juice
½ cup boiling chicken
  broth, parve
½ cup mayonnaise
¼ cup milk or Coffee Rich
2 tablespoons chopped
  parsley
1 tablespoon green onion
  or chives, minced
1 teaspoon prepared
  mustard
1½ teaspoons dried dill
  weed
¼ teaspoon pepper
7-ounce can white meat
  tuna, drained and flaked
½ cup unpeeled cucumber,
  shredded

In a large bowl, soften gelatin in lemon juice. Add broth and stir to dissolve gelatin. Add mayonnaise, milk, parsley, green onion, mustard, dill, and pepper. Beat until well mixed. Chill 30 minutes until slightly set. Then beat until frothy.

Fold in tuna and cucumber. Turn into a 2-quart mold. Chill 3 hours or overnight.

Serves 12 to 14.

# Appetizer Tuna Mold

FAVORITE RECIPES   JEWISH WOMEN'S CLUB OF BRYAN COLLEGE STATION   BRYAN, TEXAS

1 can tomato soup
⅓ cup water
2 packages unflavored
  gelatin
2 cans water-packed tuna,
  drained and flaked
3 stalks celery, chopped
1 small onion, chopped
1 medium green pepper,
  chopped
1 pound cottage cheese
1 cup Miracle Whip
1 teaspoon salt

Heat soup. Add water and gelatin and stir until gelatin is dissolved. Stir in the rest of the ingredients. Pour into a buttered fish-shaped (or other) mold. Chill until firm.

Unmold on lettuce. Serve with crackers.

Serves 16 to 18.

# Tuna Olive Antipasto

5000 YEARS IN THE KITCHEN   TEMPLE EMANUEL   DALLAS, TEXAS

1 can (7 oz.) tuna
1 can (7½ oz.) pitted olives
1 can (3 oz.) mushrooms
1 can (9 oz.) artichoke
  hearts
1 jar (8 oz.) giardiniera
  (Italian pickled
  vegetables)
1 can (8 oz.) tomato sauce
3 tablespoons salad oil
¼ cup red sweet wine
1 teaspoon salt

Drain tuna, olives, mushrooms, artichoke hearts, and giardiniera thoroughly. Mix together, using two forks so as not to mash tuna. Combine tomato sauce, oil, wine, and salt. Mix carefully with solid ingredients. Allow to stand overnight or longer.

Serve in small bowls with crackers.

Serves about 16.

*Mixture may also be used as a first course or as a filling for stuffed tomatoes, making an attractive luncheon dish. Quantities may be varied according to can sizes available.*

# Cream Puffs With Tuna Filling

IN GOOD TASTE  NATIONAL COUNCIL OF JEWISH WOMEN  CLEVELAND, OHIO

⅔ cup flour
Pinch salt
⅔ cup water
5⅓ tablespoons butter
4 eggs

*Tuna Filling*
1 can tuna (6½ oz.),
  drained
½ cup chopped celery
¼ cup chopped cucumber
4 tablespoons chopped
  sweet pickles
2 hard-cooked eggs,
  chopped
Pinch salt
Freshly ground pepper
2 tablespoons lemon juice
3 tablespoons mayonnaise

Combine flour and salt in a small bowl. Bring the water and butter to a rolling boil in a large saucepan; add all the flour at once, and beat hard with a wooden spoon until mixture pulls from the sides and forms a ball in the bottom of the pan, about 1 minute. Move the mixture to a plate, and let the pan cool down. Heat oven to 425°.

When pan is cool, return mixture to pan. Add 3 eggs, one at a time, beating well after each addition. Break the last egg into a bowl and add a teaspoon at a time until the mixture is shiny and of the consistency to drop from a spoon.

Using a pastry bag fitted with a plain round tip, pipe the mixture onto a dampened baking sheet into small mounds, 1 inch apart. Or drop by spoonfuls onto the baking sheet.

Bake in preheated oven for 20 minutes, until golden brown and crisp. Remove from oven, pierce each puff with a knife to let out steam, and return to *turned-off* oven for 10 minutes to dry out.

To make the filling, combine all the ingredients in a large bowl and chill.

Cut off tops of the puffs and fill with the tuna mixture. Replace tops and serve.

Makes  40 to 50 small puffs. Preparation time: 40 minutes.

*  The empty puffs can be stored in an air-tight container or frozen for 3 weeks.*

# Cocktail Cream Puffs

LOVE JEWISH STYLE WOMEN'S ORGANIZATION OF TEMPLE ISRAEL SOUTH ORANGE, NEW JERSEY

½ cup milk
¼ cup butter
½ cup flour, sifted
⅛ teaspoon salt
2 eggs

In a saucepan, bring milk and butter to boiling point. Add flour and salt. Cook and stir batter until it leaves the sides of the pan and forms a ball. Remove from heat and beat in eggs, one at a time. Spoon batter in small mounds on greased cookie sheet.

Bake in a 425° oven until points are light brown. Reduce heat to 325° 10 minutes.

Fill each puff and return to oven for just a minute to warm up. Cream puffs can be made in advance. (An appetizer puff should be made only bite size, not like a dessert puff.)

*Fillings:* 1. Combine mashed sardines, cream cheese, paprika, black pepper, and a little mayonnaise. 2. Combine chopped green pepper, cream cheese, seasonings. 3. Any cheese mixtures.


# Mock Lobster Salad

RECIPES BY REQUEST B'NAI SHALOM SISTERHOOD BLOUNTVILLE, TENNESSEE

2 pounds filet of halibut
2 slices lemon
1 small onion
3 pieces allspice
1 bay leaf
2 teaspoons salt
¼ teaspoon pepper
3 hard-boiled eggs,
  chopped
½ cup diced celery
½ cup chili sauce
½ cup mayonnaise
½ cup finely cut strips of
  green pepper
1 carrot, grated

Combine halibut with lemon, onion, and seasonings and steam until tender. Drain, cool, and flake.

Combine eggs, celery, chili sauce, mayonnaise, green pepper, and carrot and add to fish. Mix, correct seasonings to taste, and chill thoroughly. May be molded.

Serves 8 to 10.

# Caviar Roulade

THE WONDERFUL WORLD OF COOKING   BALDWIN HADASSAH   BALDWIN, NEW YORK

¼ cup butter or margarine
½ cup flour, sifted
2 cups milk
4 eggs, separated
4 ounces cream cheese
¼ cup light cream or milk
1 tablespoon lemon juice
2 jars (4 oz. each) red
  caviar

Grease a 10 x 15 x 1 jelly roll pan. Line bottom with waxed paper; grease and flour lightly.

Melt butter in a saucepan. Stir in the flour and cook for 1 minute. Add 2 cups milk and bring to the boiling point, stirring constantly. Cook 1 minute. Beat in egg yolks, one at a time.

In another bowl, beat egg whites until stiff; fold into yolk mixture. Spread batter in the prepared pan.

Bake for 1 hour in a 350° oven.

Blend cream cheese, cream, and lemon juice. Stir in caviar gently.

Remove cake from oven, loosen edges, and turn out onto waxed paper. Carefully peel paper from top of cake. Spread the caviar mixture evenly over the cake. Then roll up jelly roll style, starting from shorter end for a first course or from the longer end for an appetizer.

Slice about 1 inch thick and top each slice with a small amount of sour cream, if desired. May be served hot or cold.

Serves 8 as first course.

*Can be made with 1 jar of caviar instead of 2.*


# Barbecued Pecans

EDITORS' CHOICE

2 tablespoons butter
¼ cup Worcestershire
  sauce
1 tablespoon catsup
2 dashes hot sauce
4 cups pecan halves
Salt

Melt butter in large saucepan. Add Worcestershire, catsup, and hot sauce. Stir in nuts. Spoon into glass baking dish. Spread evenly.

Toast in a 400° oven about 20 minutes, stirring frequently. Turn out on absorbent towels. Sprinkle with salt.

# Pineapple and Mayonnaise Herring

EDITORS' CHOICE

1 bottle (1 qt.) herring in wine sauce (skinned)
1 can (14 oz.) pineapple chunks in own juice
1 small white onion
2 tablespoons sugar
1 teaspoon prepared mustard
1 to 1½ cups mayonnaise

Empty the herring into a colander; remove and discard the onion. Wash herring gently in cold water to remove the wine sauce flavor.

Cut herring into bite-sized pieces. Slice onion thinly, separate rings, and rinse off in cold water. Drain pineapple, reserving the juice. Cut pineapple pieces in half. Layer herring, onion, and pineapple alternately in bowl.

Mix mustard and sugar. Add mayonnaise and pineapple juice. Beat gently to mix well but do not allow to become frothy. Pour over herring making sure the sauce goes between all layers. Refrigerate overnight. Can be made 2 days before serving. Keeps up to a week.

Looks pretty served in a shallow bowl.

About 50 bite-sized pieces.


# Creamed Herring

EDITORS' CHOICE

1 bottle (1 qt.) herring in wine sauce (skinned)
3 medium onions
3 large eggs
6½ teaspoons sugar
3 teaspoons prepared mustard
1½ teaspoons white wine vinegar
2 cups sweet cream

Empty the herring into a colander; remove and discard the onion. Wash herring gently in cold water to remove the wine sauce flavor.

Cut into bite-sized pieces. Slice onions finely. Separate rings and wash in cold water. Layer herring and onion rings into bowl.

Beat eggs, sugar, mustard and vinegar in top of double boiler. Warm slowly and stir constantly — do not allow to curdle — until mixture thickens. Cool. Add cream. Pour over herring. Cover. Refrigerate overnight.

Serve with crackers, bread, and bagels.

About 50 bite-sized pieces.

# Chopped Herring

EDITORS' CHOICE

1 bottle (1 qt.) herring in
  wine sauce (skinned)
5 hard-boiled eggs
4–5 apples (not cooking
  apples), peeled and cored
2 teaspoons chopped onion
4 slices rye bread
Sugar to taste

*Garnish*
1 hard-boiled egg
Tomato
Cucumber, fresh or pickled
Parsley

Empty the herring into a colander; remove and discard the onions. Wash herring in cold water to remove the wine sauce flavor.

Grind herring, eggs, apples, onion, and rye bread finely. Feed them alternately into machine. Mix well. Taste. Add 3 to 5 tablespoons of sugar or more if you wish. Can now be frozen for a few weeks.

*To Serve:* Spread herring mixture ½-inch thick on large platter. Smooth. Separate white and yellow of egg garnish. Sieve the yellow finely and grate the white on the coarse side of the grater. Keep separate. Sprinkle yellow and white egg in a formal pattern over the surface. Surround with thinly sliced tomatoes and cucumber.

Serve with crackers or bread.

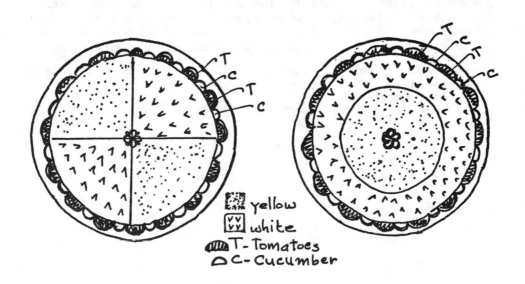

yellow
white
T - Tomatoes
C - Cucumber

# Danish Herring

1 bottle (1 qt.) herring in
  wine sauce (skinned)
⅞ cup sugar
2½ tablespoons oil

*Sauce*
1 cup peeled apple pieces
¾ cup small onion pieces
½ cup small pieces pickled
  cucumber (kosher pickles)
1½ teaspoons prepared
  mustard
1½ teaspoons ketchup
1½ cups tomato sauce
¼ cup water
¼ cup white vinegar

Empty the herring into a colander; remove and discard the onion. Wash herring gently in cold water to remove the wine sauce flavor.

Cut herring into bite-sized pieces. Place in dish and sprinkle with sugar. Add oil and toss gently to coat all pieces.

Mix together sauce ingredients and pour over herring. Refrigerate 48 hours before serving — mix gently after 24 hours. Serve in a deep bowl.

About 50 bite-sized pieces.

*\*"I usually double this recipe and store in a closed jar. Keeps 7 to 10 days. If kept longer the flavor of vinegar becomes sharper."*

# Gefilte Fish Loaf

2 pounds fish fillets
2 medium onions, cut in
  small pieces
½ cup matzo meal
1 carrot, grated
2 teaspoons oil (optional)
1 teaspoon salt
⅛ teaspoon pepper
¼ to ½ cup water

Grind fish with onion, or use food processor. Add matzo meal, carrot, oil, salt, and pepper. Mix well. Add just enough water to moisten mixture. Spoon into lightly greased loaf pan.

Bake in a 350° oven for 1 hour. Unmold on platter. Cool and serve with horseradish.

Serves about 8 as first course or 16 as appetizer.

*\* Serve sliced as a first course or cubed on toothpicks as an appetizer.*

# Chopped Liver

KOSHER COOKERY UNLIMITED   WOMEN'S LEAGUE FOR CONSERVATIVE JUDAISM   NEW YORK, NEW YORK

1 pound liver (chicken,
  beef, or calves)
¼ cup rendered chicken
  fat (or other shortening)
1 medium onion
2 hard-boiled eggs
Salt and pepper to taste

Broil liver 5 to 10 minutes until light brown on both sides. Fry onion in chicken fat till nicely browned. Put liver and onions through food chopper with eggs, using fine cutting blade. Combine with the remaining fat, and salt and pepper to taste.

Serve on lettuce leaf garnished with radish, olive, or pickle.

Makes about 2 cups.

*Or serve with crackers. May add more onion or egg to taste.*

# Hot canapes

## Kiki's Appetizer

POT OF GOLD  SISTERHOOD CONGREGATION HAR SHALOM  POTOMAC, MARYLAND

1 can (4½ oz.) black
  chopped olives
¼ cup sliced green onions
  (scallions)
2 tablespoons chopped
  fresh parsley
4 tablespoons mayonnaise
  or salad dressing
¼ teaspoon curry powder
Pinch salt
8 slices white bread,
  toasted (use "square"
  sandwich bread)
¾ cup shredded Cheddar
  cheese

Combine olives, onions, parsley, mayonnaise, curry powder, and salt. Spread on toast. Sprinkle with shredded cheese. Cut each slice in quarters and arrange on cookie sheet.

Broil until cheese melts and bubbles. Serve immediately, although this still tastes delicious even when cool.

*Notes:* you can make these several hours ahead and refrigerate until time to broil and serve. Recipe can be doubled or tripled as needed; allow at least 1 whole slice of bread per person. If you're running low on cheese, a few shreds are all that is really necessary per piece, especially if you are using sharp Cheddar. It makes a very pretty combination.

Makes 32 pieces.

* *Be sure to make enough; these go fast and everyone asks for more!*

# Quick and Easy Appetizer
POT OF GOLD  SISTERHOOD CONGREGATION HAR SHALOM  POTOMAC, MARYLAND

10 thin slices white bread
1 cup mayonnaise
7 tablespoons grated
  Parmesan cheese (or
  more)
1 bunch scallions, chopped
  fine (white part only)

Toast bread; trim crusts and cut into quarters. Combine mayonnaise, cheese, and scallions. Spread on bread. Arrange on cookie sheet and broil just until lightly browned; serve hot.

Makes 40.


# Swiss Sandwich Puffs
CLEARWATER COOKS  TEMPLE B'NAI ISRAEL SISTERHOOD  CLEARWATER, FLORIDA

16 slices party rye bread
½ cup mayonnaise
¼ cup finely chopped
  onion
2 tablespoons parsley
8 slices processed Swiss
  cheese
Black olives (pitted), sliced

Lightly toast both sides of bread. Combine mayonnaise, onion, and parsley; spread on toast. Cut out rounds of cheese to fit the bread and place on top of mixture. Broil 3 to 4 inches from heat until cheese is puffy and golden. Decorate with sliced olives.

Makes 16 puffs.


# Easy Blintza-Type Appetizer
RODEPH SHALOM SISTERHOOD COOKBOOK  RODEPH SHALOM SISTERHOOD  PHILADELPHIA, PENNSYLVANIA

1 loaf white bread, sliced
12-ounces pot cheese (or
  farmers cheese)
1 egg, slightly beaten
¼ teaspoon salt
Dash pepper
Melted butter
Garlic powder

Remove crust and roll out bread slices with a rolling pin. Combine remaining ingredients and mix well. Place about a tablespoonful of cheese mixture down the center of each slice of bread. Brush the edges of the bread with melted butter; roll up and press together, then cut in half. Place, seam side down, on a shallow, well-greased pan. Brush tops with butter and sprinkle with garlic powder.

Bake in a preheated 400° oven until golden brown. Serve hot.

Makes about 20.

* Can be made ahead and placed in refrigerator or frozen. If frozen, defrost completely before baking.

# Cheese Straws

ARTISTRY IN THE KITCHEN   TEMPLE WOMEN'S ASSOCIATION   CLEVELAND, OHIO

1 cup flour, sifted
¼ teaspoon salt
½ cup butter or margarine
2 tablespoons ice water
½ cup grated sharp
  Cheddar cheese

Sift flour and salt together. Cut in butter. Add water and mix with fork until mixture sticks together.

Roll out on a floured board. Sprinkle with ⅓ of the cheese and fold over. Roll out again, sprinkle with ⅓ of the cheese, and fold over. Repeat once more.

Cut into 2-inch x ½-inch strips and place on an ungreased cookie sheet.

Bake in a 425° oven for 12 minutes. Serve hot.

Makes 3 dozen.

# Crisp Parmesan Strips

DELECTABLE COLLECTABLES   SISTERHOOD OF TEMPLE JUDEA   TARZANA, CALIFORNIA

12 slices white bread
1 cup melted butter or
  margarine
1½ cups grated Parmesan
  cheese
Paprika

Trim crusts off bread and cut into 4 strips per slice. Dip one side lightly into melted butter, then in cheese. Place strips (cheese side up) ½ inch apart on a cookie sheet.

Bake in a 400° oven 8 to 10 minutes or until golden brown. Remove strips from pan and place on wire rack; sprinkle with paprika. Serve warm.

Makes 48.

# Cheese Puffs With Mustard

THE SPICE OF LIFE   B'NAI B'RITH WOMEN   UNION, NEW JERSEY

6-ounce roll sharp cheese
½ cup butter
1 egg yolk
½ teaspoon dry mustard
Grated onion, to taste
Worcestershire sauce, to
  taste
16 slices day-old bread

Mix all ingredients, except bread, until the consistency of soft butter. Spread about ½ the mixture on 8 slices of bread. Top with other 8 bread slices. Cut off crusts and cut each sandwich into quarters. Frost tops and sides with remaining cheese mix. Place on buttered cookie sheet. Cover and freeze.

When ready to use, remove from freezer and place in a preheated 350° oven for 10 to 12 minutes or until brownish and puffed.

Makes 32 puffs.

# Dorothy's Cheese Rounds

MEASURES AND TREASURES   TEMPLE BETH EL SISTERHOOD   DAYTONA BEACH, FLORIDA

1 cup sharp Cheddar
  cheese, grated
1 cup butter or margarine
1 package onion soup mix
2 cups all-purpose flour

Combine cheese, butter, and onion soup mix; work in the flour with your hands or a pastry blender. Form into 3 or 4 rolls. Place in refrigerator overnight.

Slice and bake in a 375° oven for 10 to 15 minutes. Rolls may be frozen unbaked for future use.

* If cheese is too soft to grate easily, put it in the freezer for a few minutes.

# Fish Toast

ELEGANT ESSEN  SISTERHOOD OF JEWISH CENTER  EAST NORTHPORT, NEW YORK

1 pound raw fish (sole is good)
1 onion
1 can (8 oz.) water chestnuts
1 egg
1 teaspoon sugar, or more to taste
1½ tablespoons flour
Salt to taste
13–15 slices day-old white bread, thin slices, crusts removed
Oil for frying

Grind together fish, onion, and water chestnuts. Mix with egg, sugar, flour, and salt. Pull 1 or 2 slices bread into bits, and add enough to bind mixture together.

Cut remaining bread into 4 triangles. Spread each triangle with 1 heaping teaspoon of the fish mixture.

Heat the oil (about ¾-inch deep) to 365°. Gently lower the bread into the oil with the fish side down. Fry the first side for 1 minute and the other side for a few seconds until golden brown. Fry only a few at a time.

Drain and serve or freeze. To defrost, bake at 375° for 10 to 12 minutes.

Makes 48 to 56 pieces.

* This recipe is not difficult if you have an electric grinder or food processor.

# Toasted Mushroom Rolls

SISTERHOOD CHOICE  TEMPLE EMANUEL SISTERHOOD  EDISON, NEW JERSEY

½ pound mushrooms
¼ to ½ cup butter
3 tablespoons flour
¾ teaspoon salt
1 cup light cream
2 teaspoons minced chives
1 teaspoon lemon juice
1 family-size loaf white bread, sliced

Clean mushrooms and chop finely. In a large frying pan, melt butter and sauté mushrooms for 5 minutes. Mix together flour and salt and blend with mushrooms. Stir in cream. Cook until thick. Then add chives and lemon juice. Cool.

Remove crusts from bread and roll slices thin. Spread with mixture and roll up. (May be packed and frozen before toasting. Defrost before toasting.)

When ready to serve, cut each roll in half or thirds and toast on all sides in a 400° oven.

Makes about 42 pieces.

# Mock Egg Rollups

CREATIVE COOKERY  TEMPLE SHAARE TEFILAH  NORWOOD, MASSACHUSETTS

¼ pound ground veal
½ bunch celery, chopped
3 onions, chopped
3 green peppers, chopped
1 can mushrooms, chopped
½ can bean sprouts,
  drained (16 oz. can)
Salt, pepper, soy sauce,
  and garlic to taste
1 large loaf white bread,
  thin sliced
Margarine (pareve), melted

Sauté the veal and all vegetables until brown. Add spices and mix well. Cut all crust from bread, and roll each piece very thin. Fill with about 1 tablespoon filling and roll up. Dip in margarine.

Bake in a 350° oven for 20 minutes or until golden. Can freeze baked or unbaked.

Makes about 2 dozen.

# French Toasted Liver Sandwiches

THE HAPPY COOKER  SISTERHOOD OF MALVERNE JEWISH CENTER  MALVERNE, NEW YORK

½ pound prepared
  chopped liver
1 loaf sliced white bread,
  crusts removed
4 eggs, beaten
⅓ cup water
Oil for frying

Spread chopped liver on ½ of the bread slices; top with remaining slices to form sandwiches. Cut each sandwich into 4 triangles. Combine eggs and water. Dip each triangle into egg-water mixture and fry until brown on both sides.

Makes about 56 small sandwiches.

# Hot appetizers

## Felafel

THE HAPPY COOKER  SISTERHOOD OF MALVERNE JEWISH CENTER  MALVERNE, NEW YORK

2 cups canned chick-peas,
  drained
2 cups fine dry bread
  crumbs
½ teaspoon chopped
  parsley
½ teaspoon salt
¼ teaspoon (or more)
  curry powder
¼ teaspoon pepper
2 eggs, beaten
2 tablespoons melted butter
  or margarine
Extra bread crumbs
Shortening for deep frying
Syrian bread
Lettuce, chopped
Tomatoes, chopped
Cucumbers, chopped

*Techina Sauce*
1 can techina sauce
Lemon juice
Salad oil or olive oil

Mash the chick-peas, then add bread crumbs, parsley, salt, curry powder, and pepper. Stir thoroughly to mix. Add eggs; stir in melted butter. Shape into ½ to ¾ inch balls and roll in extra crumbs.

Fry a few at a time in hot, deep fat for 2 or 3 minutes until golden brown. Remove with a slotted spoon and drain on absorbent paper.

Dilute techina sauce with a little lemon juice and a little oil until it is the consistency of thin sour cream.

Cut off one end of the Syrian bread to form a pocket; fill pocket with lettuce, tomatoes, cucumbers, and hot felafel balls, then add some of the techina sauce.

This recipe makes 15 felafel balls.

# Knishes

BALABUSTAS — MORE FAVORITE RECIPES  B'NAI ISRAEL SISTERHOOD  GAINESVILLE, FLORIDA

2 cups flour
½ teaspoon baking powder
¼ teaspoon salt
1 egg
¼ cup oil
6 tablespoons warm water

*Potato Filling*
4 cooked potatoes, mashed
3 onions (approximately)
  chopped and fried crisp
2 eggs
Melted chicken fat, to taste
Salt and pepper to taste

*Liver Filling*
½ pound liver, broiled and
  chopped fine
3 broiled chicken livers,
  chopped
½ pound ground beef,
  cooked
½ cup mashed potatoes
1 egg
1 onion, minced and
  browned in oil
1 tablespoon oil
½ teaspoon salt
Dash *each* cinnamon and
  pepper

Sift flour, baking powder, and salt into a bowl. Beat egg, oil, and water and add to the flour mixture. Knead lightly until dough is soft; it will be slightly oily but not sticky. Cover and set in a warm place for at least 1 hour.

Make filling. For either filling, combine all ingredients and mix well.

Divide dough in half and roll as thin as possible into a rectangle. Spread the filling on long side of the dough and roll like a jelly roll. Cut into 1-inch slices. Pull ends of the dough over the filling and tuck into the knish to form small cakes. Place on a well-greased baking sheet.

Bake in a 375° oven until brown and crisp.

Makes about 3 dozen.

# Chicken Liver and Cracker Kugel

ESSEN 'N FRESSEN  CONGREGATION BETH CHAIM  EAST WINDSOR, NEW JERSEY

3 large onions, diced
¾ to 1 pound chicken
  livers
Oil, for frying
20 ounces Ritz-type
  crackers (1-pound box
  plus handful)
2 cans condensed chicken
  rice soup (undiluted)
3 eggs

Sauté onions until light brown and remove from pan. Broil the liver. Chop together with onion.

Crumble crackers (not too fine) in a large bowl. Add soup and eggs; mix. Combine with onions and liver. Put into a 9 x 13 ungreased pan.

Bake in a 350° oven for 30 to 45 minutes or until top is crispy. Can be served hot or at room temperature.

Serves 12 to 14.

# Chicken Liver Strudel Slices

WHAT'S COOKING IN BIRMINGHAM   B'NAI B'RITH WOMEN   BIRMINGHAM, ALABAMA

1 onion, finely chopped
6 tablespoons margarine
1 pound chicken livers,
  washed and drained
¼ pound fresh mushrooms,
  sliced
2 tablespoons cognac
¼ cup soft bread crumbs
Salt and black pepper
1 egg, lightly beaten
⅛ teaspoon allspice
2 tablespoons chopped
  parsley
¼ pound (approx.) phyllo
  pastry
Melted margarine

In a small skillet, sauté onion in 2 tablespoons margarine until tender but not browned. Add remaining margarine and livers. Cook quickly until browned on all sides. Add mushrooms and cook 3 minutes longer.

Turn liver mixture onto a chopping board and chop until fine. Scrape into a bowl and add cognac, bread crumbs, salt, pepper, egg, allspice, and parsley. Mix. Allow to cool.

Place 2 sheets of phyllo pastry on damp cloth; brush with melted margarine. Top with 2 more sheets of pastry; brush with margarine and top with 2 more sheets. More sheets of pastry, up to a total of 10, may be used if desired.

Mold liver mixture into a sausage shape along the long side of the pastry and roll up. Lift carefully and place, seam side down, on a baking sheet (preferably one with low sides in case fat oozes out while baking).

Bake in a 375° oven until pastry is crisp and golden, 30 to 40 minutes. Cut into ½-inch slices and serve immediately.

To freeze, wrap in aluminum foil after cooking. Remove from freezer ½ hour before serving. Thaw for 10 to 15 minutes, then slice and bake at 375° for 15 minutes or until heated through.

Makes 18 to 24 slices.

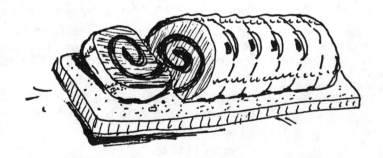

# Rumaki

WORLD OF OUR FLAVORS   BETH HILLEL CONGREGATION   WILMETTE, ILLINOIS

1 pound chicken livers,
   broiled
1 can water chestnuts
½ cup teriyaki sauce
2 pounds beef frye

Marinate chicken livers and water chestnuts in teriyaki sauce overnight. Drain the livers and cut in half. Place one water chestnut on each piece of liver and wrap with a strip of beef frye.

Bake in a 350° oven for 40 to 60 minutes or until done.

Makes approximately 30 appetizers.

*\* Prunes stuffed with walnuts may be substituted for chicken livers and chestnuts.*

# Stuffed Cabbage

COOK ALONG WITH US   SISTERHOOD OF TEMPLE BETH SHALOM   PEABODY, MASSACHUSETTS

1 large head cabbage
1 pound ground beef
½ cup instant rice (raw)
1 onion, grated
2 eggs
1 teaspoon salt
¼ teaspoon pepper
1 large onion, sliced
2 cans (No. 2½) whole
   tomatoes
2 cans (8 oz. *each*) tomato
   sauce
Juice of 2 lemons
1 teaspoon salt
¼ teaspoon pepper
½ to 1 cup brown sugar

Remove 12 large leaves from cabbage. Shave off thick part of each leaf. Pour on boiling water to soften leaves.

Combine meat, rice, grated onion, eggs, salt, and pepper. Place mound of meat mixture on each leaf. Loosely fold over the two sides of each leaf and roll up.

In bottom of large, deep, oven-proof pan, place several remaining cabbage leaves. Cover with layers of stuffed leaves, seam side down, and onion slices. Add tomatoes, tomato sauce, lemon juice, salt, pepper, and sugar to taste. Bring to a boil.

Bake, covered, in a 350° oven for 1 hour. Cook uncovered for an additional 1 hour or until done.

Serves 12 as a first course; use smaller cabbage leaves to make 24 or more bite-sized appetizers.

*\* Place cored head of cabbage in freezer for at least 8 hours, and it will become soft enough to use without blanching.*

# Meat Kugel Appetizer

SUPER CHEF  BETH ISRAEL TEMPLE CENTER  WARREN, OHIO

8 ounces fine noodles
  (little less)
1½ pounds ground meat
3 small onions, diced
3-4 tablespoons oil
5 large eggs, separated
1 package Lipton's onion
  soup mix
Cornflake crumbs
Salt and pepper to taste

Cook the noodles. Brown onions and meat in 1 to 2 tablespoons oil; drain fat. Beat egg whites and set aside.

In mixing bowl, combine noodles, meat, and onions. Add ½ the dry soup mix and the egg yolks; mix well. Fold in beaten egg whites. Pour mixture into a 9 x 13 pan heated with 2 tablespoons oil. Top with a mixture of the cornflake crumbs and the other ½ of the soup mix.

Bake in a 325° oven for 45 minutes. Cut into very small squares.

Serves 15 to 20.

# Sweet and Sour Meat Balls I

THE HAPPY COOKER OF TEMPLE SHALOM  TEMPLE SHALOM  WEST NEWTON, MASSACHUSETTS

3 slices white bread, crusts
  removed
2 pounds ground beef
1 egg, beaten
1 small onion, minced
1 clove garlic, minced
1 teaspoon salt
½ teaspoon pepper
1 teaspoon paprika
½ tablespoon thyme
¼ cup beef broth

*Sauce*
1 can (1 lb.) Italian
  tomatoes, drained
⅓ cup sugar
⅓ cup brown sugar
4 ginger snaps, crumbled
Juice of 1½ lemons
Salt

Soak bread in water. Squeeze. Combine ground beef with the egg, onion, garlic, and seasonings. Blend in broth. Form into small balls.

*Sauce:* Sieve tomatoes; discard seeds. Mix with remaining ingredients and heat in a large saucepan. Add meat balls and simmer about 30 minutes, until sauce thickens slightly.

Meat balls and sauce may be frozen.

Makes about 100 one-inch meatballs.

# Sweet and Sour Meat Balls II

FOOD FOR THOUGHT  TEMPLE BETH EL  FT. PIERCE, FLORIDA

1 pound ground beef
1 can (16 oz.) whole berry
  cranberry sauce
1 can (8 oz.) Arturo sauce
  (or other spicy tomato
  sauce)
Pinch cinnamon

Shape meat into bite-size balls.

Combine cranberry sauce and tomato sauce in a saucepan. Add cinnamon. Put meat balls into pan, and cook over low heat for 30 to 45 minutes. Great!

Serves 4 to 5 as appetizers.

Makes about forty 1-inch balls.


# Sweet and Sour Meatballs III

ARTISTRY IN THE KITCHEN  TEMPLE WOMEN'S ASSOCIATION  CLEVELAND, OHIO

1 pound ground chuck
1 egg
Salt to taste
1 medium onion, thinly
  sliced
½ cup white sugar
½ cup dark raisins
½ teaspoon sour salt

Combine chuck, egg, and salt. Form into small balls.

Sauté onion and sugar in frying pan; stir over low heat until onions are golden brown and sugar is absorbed. Add raisins and sour salt. Drop meatballs into onion-raisin mixture and stew over low heat for 1 hour.

Serve in a chafing dish.

Makes about 40.


# Sauerkraut Balls

FAIRMONT TEMPLE COOKBOOK  FAIRMONT TEMPLE SISTERHOOD  CLEVELAND, OHIO

1 pound ground beef
1 large can sauerkraut, well
  drained
1 medium onion
2 tablespoons flour
2 eggs
½ to 1 cup mashed
  potatoes
Cracker crumbs

Put meat, sauerkraut, and onion through food chopper. Add flour, eggs and potatoes. Mix well.

Form into 1-inch balls and roll in cracker crumbs. Deep fry and serve hot.

Makes about 50 meatballs.

# Cocktail Meatballs in Barbecue Dip

THE KOSHER KITCHEN   TEMPLE SHAAREY ZEDEK SISTERHOOD   BUFFALO, NEW YORK

1 pound hamburger
1 egg, slightly beaten
1 cup water
2 tablespoons grated onion
1 cup matzo meal or bread
  crumbs
1½ teaspoons salt
¼ teaspoon pepper
2 tablespoons cooking oil

Sauce
¼ cup minced onion
2 tablespoons margarine
  (parve)
½ cup chili sauce
1 can (8 oz.) tomato sauce
1 can (4½ oz.) chopped
  ripe olives, optional
2 teaspoons horseradish
1 teaspoon dry mustard
1 teaspoon chili powder
1 teaspoon Worcestershire
  sauce
¼ teaspoon Tabasco

Combine hamburger, egg, water, onion, matzo meal, salt and pepper, and form into tiny balls. Brown in oil.

*Sauce:* Sauté onion in margarine until soft. Do not brown. Stir in remaining ingredients. Blend well and place in serving dish.

Arrange meatballs on platter with sauce. Serve with toothpicks.

Makes about 40 one-inch meatballs.

*Meatballs may be made in advance and frozen. Freeze in a single layer on wax paper, then pack in plastic bags. At serving time, reheat in a 350° oven for 20 to 30 minutes.*

# Frank Puffs

FAVORITE RECIPES   MONMOUTH REFORM TEMPLE   TINTON FALLS, NEW JERSEY

1 cup pancake mix
½ teaspoon onion powder
½ teaspoon dry mustard
¼ teaspoon salt
¾ cup water
8-ounce package cocktail
  franks
Fat for deep frying

*Sauce*
¼ cup brown sugar, firmly
  packed
1 tablespoon cornstarch
¼ cup pineapple juice
¼ cup vinegar
1 tablespoon catsup
1 tablespoon soy sauce
4 drops Tabasco

Combine pancake mix, onion powder, mustard, and salt in a bowl. Add water and stir until fairly smooth.

Cut weiners in half. Dry on paper toweling so batter will cling well. Dip into batter and fry in hot (400°) deep fat for 2½ to 3 minutes, turning once. Drain on cookie sheets.

Heat in a preheated 425° oven for about 8 minutes. Serve hot with sauce.

Makes about 16.

*Sauce:* Mix together sauce ingredients in a pan and cook until smooth and clear.

# Barbeque Chicken Wings

THE KOSHER KITCHEN   TEMPLE SHAAREY ZEDEK SISTERHOOD   BUFFALO, NEW YORK

1 small can (6 oz.) frozen
  orange juice concentrate
6 ounces soy sauce
6 ounces prepared mustard
2 pounds chicken wings

Combine orange juice, soy sauce, and mustard. Place chicken wings in a single layer in shallow pan. Pour liquid mixture over chicken.

Place under broiler until brown, turning when necessary. When both sides are browned, bake in 300° oven until most of sauce is gone (approximately 1 hour). Refrigerate overnight and reheat for serving.

Serves about 20.

# Chicken Nuggets With Spicy Sauces

THE SPORT OF COOKING  WOMEN'S AMERICAN ORT, VII  CLEVELAND, OHIO

6 whole chicken breasts,
  skinned and boned
2 eggs, beaten
1 cup water
1½ teaspoons salt
3 tablespoons sesame seeds
1 cup flour
1 to 1½ pints corn oil

Cut chicken into 1 x 1½ inch nuggets. You can get 6 pieces from each half of a 12 to 14 ounce breast. Mix eggs, water, salt, sesame seeds, and flour into a batter.

Pour oil into a heavy 3-quart saucepan or deep fryer, filling no more than ⅓ full. Heat to 375°.

Dip the chicken nuggets into the batter; drain off excess batter. Fry 3 to 5 minutes or until golden brown. (Fry 8 or 9 at a time in a single layer.) Drain on paper towels. Serve with trio of sauces.

Makes 72 pieces.

*Nippy Pineapple Sauce:* Mix 1 jar (12 oz.) pineapple preserves, ¼ cup prepared mustard, and ¼ cup prepared horseradish in a saucepan and heat.

*Dill Sauce:* Mix together ½ cup sour cream, ½ cup mayonnaise, 1 teaspoon dried dill weed, and 2 tablespoons finely chopped dill pickle. Let flavors blend for several hours before serving.

*Royalty Sauce:* Mix 1 cup catsup, ½ teaspoon dry mustard, 1 tablespoon brown sugar, 2 tablespoons vinegar, and 6 tablespoons margarine in a saucepan, and cook 4 to 5 minutes, stirring constantly.

# Chinese Egg Rolls
FROM THE KOSHER KITCHENS OF BETH ISRAEL  BETH ISRAEL SISTERHOOD  MILWAUKEE, WISCONSIN

2 cups flour
2 tablespoons cornstarch
1 tablespoon salt
1 teaspoon sugar
1 egg, beaten
2 cups water
Oil for frying

*Filling*
4 cups cabbage
½ cup green onions
½ cup celery
1 pound ground beef
¼ cup oil or Marparv
1 small can bean sprouts
¼ cup soy sauce
2 tablespoons sugar
1 teaspoon salt

Sift flour, cornstarch, and salt; add sugar and beaten egg. Gradually beat in water until a smooth, thin batter is formed.

Lightly grease a 6-inch skillet with oil. Pour about 4 tablespoons of the batter into the center of the pan. Tilt the pan rapidly to spread batter over the entire surface. Cook over low heat until edges pull away from the sides. Gently turn pancake and cook other side slightly. Remove from pan and continue until all batter is used.

Place a heaping tablespoon of filling in the center of each pancake. Spread to within ½ inch of edge. Roll, folding in the sides, and seal edge with a mixture of 1 tablespoon flour and 2 tablespoons water.

Fry egg rolls in deep hot fat (360°) until golden brown. Serve hot with mustard sauce. May be frozen and reheated in a hot oven before serving.

*Filling:* Shred cabbage fine and cook in boiling water for 3 minutes. Drain. Chop onions and celery fine and add to cabbage. In a large skillet, brown beef in oil. Add vegetables and seasonings and cook for 5 minutes. Drain and cool.

Yield: 12 to 15 egg rolls.

# Bite-Size Spinach Egg Foo Yong

FROM CHARLESTON WITH LOVE   SYNAGOGUE EMANU-EL SISTERHOOD   CHARLESTON, SOUTH CAROLINA

3 eggs, slightly beaten
½ 10-ounce package frozen chopped spinach, cooked and drained
½ cup finely chopped water chestnuts
¼ cup finely chopped green pepper
¼ cup finely chopped onion
¼ teaspoon salt
Dash pepper

Brown Sauce
2 tablespoons butter
4 teaspoons cornstarch
2 teaspoons sugar
1 cup water
3 tablespoons soy sauce

Combine eggs, spinach, water chestnuts, green pepper, onion, salt, and pepper; mix well. Drop from teaspoon onto hot, well-greased griddle. Brown on both sides over medium-high heat.

Serve on a warming tray with Brown Sauce.

To prepare ahead, place pieces on baking sheet, cover, and chill. Before serving, heat in a 300° oven for 20 to 25 minutes.

*Brown Sauce:* In a small saucepan, melt butter. Stir in cornstarch, sugar, water, and soy sauce. Cook and stir until thick and bubbly. Makes 1⅓ cups sauce.

Makes 3 dozen.

# Spinach Balls

WORLD OF OUR FLAVORS   BETH HILLEL CONGREGATION   WILMETTE, ILLINOIS

2 packages (10 oz. *each*) frozen chopped spinach
2 cups herb stuffing mix
1 cup grated Parmesan cheese
6 eggs, beaten
¾ cup butter, softened
Salt and pepper to taste

Cook spinach according to directions on package; drain well. Combine all ingredients and roll into walnut size balls.

Bake in a 350° oven for 10 minutes.

Makes 70 to 80.

\* *To freeze, place on cookie sheet. When frozen, transfer to a plastic bag until ready to use. Frozen balls do not have to be defrosted before baking. Just increase the baking time a few minutes.*

# Spinach Cheese Squares

QUICK AND EASY COOKBOOK   MAIN LINE REFORM TEMPLE SISTERHOOD   WYNNEWOOD, PENNSYLVANIA

4 tablespoons butter
3 eggs
1 cup flour
1 cup milk
1 teaspoon salt
1 teaspoon baking powder
1 pound Monterey Jack cheese (or other mild cheese), grated
2 packages frozen chopped spinach, thawed and drained

Preheat oven to 350°. In a 9 x 13 baking pan, melt the butter in the oven. Remove from oven.

In a large mixing bowl, beat the eggs, then add the flour, milk, salt, and baking powder. Mix well. Add the cheese and spinach. Pour into the baking pan.

Bake in a 350° oven for 35 minutes. Remove from oven. Cool for 45 minutes in order to set. Cut into bite-sized squares.

Makes 25 appetizers.

*To freeze: Place squares on a cookie sheet and freeze, then transfer into plastic bags. Before serving, remove from bags, place on cookie sheet, heat in 325° oven for 12 minutes.*

# Spinach Cheese Pastries

KNISHES, GEFILTE FISHES AND OTHER JEWISH DISHES   TEMPLE ISRAEL SISTERHOOD   TALLAHASSEE, FLORIDA

8 ounces cream cheese, softened
1 cup butter or margarine, softened
2 cups flour, sifted

*Filling*
1 onion, finely chopped
3 tablespoons olive oil
1 package frozen chopped spinach, thawed and well-drained
1 teaspoon salt
¼ pound feta cheese, crumbled
4 ounces pot cheese
1 egg, beaten

With a fork, mix cream cheese and butter. Cut in the flour. Work with hands until dough holds together. Place on waxed paper, form into a ball, and chill overnight. Roll out dough ⅓-inch thick with floured rolling pin on a well-floured surface. Cut into 2-inch rounds.

*Filling:* Sauté onion in oil until softened; add spinach and salt. Cook over low heat until tender. Mix cheeses together and stir in egg. Add spinach mixture and blend well.

Place a little spinach filling on each round and fold over. Moisten edge so it will hold together. Flute edge with a fork and prick center. Place pastries on a cookie sheet.

Bake in a 425° oven for 15 minutes or until golden brown. Serve warm.

Makes 70 to 100 small pastries.

*Pastries can be frozen unbaked. Any leftover spinach-cheese mixture may be used in an omelet.*

# Champinones Adobados
# (Marinated Mushrooms)

DELECTABLE COLLECTABLES  SISTERHOOD OF TEMPLE JUDEA  TARZANA, CALIFORNIA

½ cup butter
1 small onion, finely
chopped
½ pound small fresh
mushrooms (or one 8 oz.
jar mushrooms, drained)
1 teaspoon oregano,
crushed
½ teaspoon *each* salt, garlic
salt, and thyme
½ teaspoon hot sauce
2 tablespoons fresh lime
juice
¼ cup dry sherry

Melt butter in large skillet. Add onion and sauté until clear. Add mushrooms and coat well. Add herbs. Sprinkle remaining ingredients over all and stir to mix well. Cover pan and simmer until liquid is gone and mushrooms are dry.

Serve warm with toothpicks.

* *You may find, as we did, that ¼ cup butter is sufficient.*

# Stuffed Mushrooms Grandmere

THE HAPPY COOKER  SISTERHOOD OF MALVERNE JEWISH CENTER  MALVERNE, NEW YORK

24 medium-to-large
mushrooms
6 tablespoons butter or
margarine
2 cloves garlic, crushed
½ cup wheat germ
½ cup seasoned bread
crumbs (packaged), or
white or whole wheat
crumbs with extra salt
½ cup grated Parmesan
cheese
2 tablespoons minced
parsley
Vegetable salt and Spike
pepper* to taste

Wash mushrooms well. Remove stems and chop. Sauté caps briefly in 2 tablespoons butter; place in a buttered baking dish.

Melt another 2 tablespoons margarine in same skillet and sauté chopped mushroom stems and garlic. Blend in wheat germ, bread crumbs, Parmesan cheese, parsley, and salt and pepper to taste.

Fill mushroom caps generously with crumb mixture. Melt 2 tablespoons butter and drizzle over tops.

Bake in a 350° oven for 15 to 20 minutes.

Serves 6 to 8.

* *Spike pepper is available in health food stores.*

# Stuffed Mushrooms

GOLDEN SOUP  AHAVATH ACHIM SISTERHOOD  ATLANTA, GEORGIA

½ pound fresh mushrooms
2 tablespoons melted butter
4 tablespoons soft butter
1 small clove garlic,
  crushed
3 tablespoons Monterey
  Jack cheese, finely diced
  or shredded
2 tablespoons red wine
1 teaspoon soy sauce
⅓ cup fine cracker crumbs

Remove stems from mushrooms. Brush mushroom caps with melted butter.

Combine soft butter with garlic and cheese. Add wine, soy sauce, and crumbs to make a paste. Fill caps. Place on foil-covered cookie sheet, and place under broiler for 3 minutes.

Makes about 16.

*Absolutely delicious and simple to make.*

# Mushroom Turnovers

TO SERVE WITH LOVE  SISTERHOOD OF TEMPLE AVODA  FAIRLAWN, NEW JERSEY

9 ounces cream cheese
½ cup butter or margarine
1½ cups flour

*Filling*
3 tablespoons butter
½ pound fresh
  mushrooms, chopped
1 large onion, chopped
¼ teaspoon thyme
½ teaspoon salt
Dash pepper
2 tablespoons flour
¼ cup light cream

Combine cream cheese, ½ cup butter, and 1½ cups flour. Blend well and chill for 1 hour.

Melt 3 tablespoons butter, add mushrooms and onions; cook, stirring, for a few minutes. Add seasonings, sprinkle with 2 tablespoons flour. Mix well. Stir in the cream, and cook very gently until thickened (few minutes). Set aside to cool.

Remove dough from refrigerator and roll out to ⅛-inch thickness. Cut into 2½-inch rounds. Place 1 teaspoon filling in center of each circle. Fold dough in half and pinch ends. Prick with fork. Freeze at this point, if desired.

Bake in a 450° for 15 minutes, or place under broiler.

Makes about 20.

# Artichokes and Cheese

GARDEN OF EATING  SISTERHOOD TEMPLE BETH OR  CLARK, NEW JERSEY

2 jars (6 oz. each)
  marinated artichoke
  hearts
1 small onion, chopped
  fine
1 clove garlic, minced (or
  ½ teaspoon garlic
  powder)
4 eggs, lightly beaten
2 cups shredded sharp
  cheese
¼ cup bread crumbs
2 tablespoons dried parsley
¼ teaspoon salt
⅛ teaspoon pepper
⅛ teaspoon oregano
½ teaspoon Tabasco

Drain oil from one jar of artichoke hearts into frying pan. Drain oil from second jar and discard. Chop the artichokes.

Sauté onion and garlic for 5 minutes. Combine remaining ingredients and add to pan. Mix. Lightly press into an 8 x 8 baking dish.

Bake in a 325° oven for 30 minutes or until set. Can be frozen.

Makes about 15 pieces.

# Tiropitta (Cheese Triangles)

ONE MORE BITE  TEMPLE BETH ISRAEL SISTERHOOD  SAN DIEGO, CALIFORNIA

½ pound feta cheese
4 ounces cream cheese
2 tablespoons grated
  Parmesan cheese
2 eggs
1 box (16 oz.) filo dough
½ cup melted butter
Oil

Mix the cheeses and eggs well with the mixer.

Cut one sheet of filo the long way into 2-inch strips. (Keep all the rest of the filo covered with a damp cloth or towel.) Mix butter with some oil and brush onto a filo strip. Place a teaspoon of the cheese mixture in a corner and fold it over in a triangle, repeating until you reach the end of the strip, like folding a flag. Brush some butter-oil on the top.

Repeat with each strip until all the cheese is used. Place on a cookie sheet.

Bake in a 350° oven for 15 to 20 minutes until brown and crispy.

Makes 60 to 70 triangles.

* This takes time to prepare but is nice for a special occasion.

# Miniature Potato Latkes

4 large potatoes
2 eggs, beaten
1 teaspoon salt
1 tablespoon flour
2 tablespoons onion, grated
½ teaspoon baking powder
1 teaspoon lemon juice

Cut potatoes in small pieces. Put all ingredients in blender or food processor and blend. Let sit for 15 minutes. Spoon liquid off top. (Potatoes may be grated by hand.)

Drop mixture by teaspoonfuls onto hot greased skillet. Brown well on both sides. Serve immediately or freeze.

To freeze, place between sheets of aluminum foil in single layers using a cookie sheet as a base. To serve, heat one layer of latkes at a time right on its aluminum foil sheet in a 450° oven for 5 minutes. Keep warm on hot tray and serve with apple sauce and sour cream for dipping.

Makes about 5 dozen.

# Miniature Quiche

½ cup butter
3 ounces cream cheese
1 cup flour (unsifted)

*Filling*
1 egg, slightly beaten
½ cup milk
¼ teaspoon salt
1 cup grated Cheddar
  cheese

Work the butter, cream cheese, and flour together; form into a ball. Flatten the ball, use a knife to score into 24 sections, then form into 24 little balls. Press each ball into one cup of a mini muffin tin. Cover with plastic wrap and refrigerate overnight.

Combine filling ingredients and pour into the prepared shells.

Bake in a preheated 350° oven for 30 minutes. When cool, freeze on cookie sheet and put into a plastic bag. To reheat, bake in a preheated 450° oven for 10 minutes.

Makes 24 pieces.

*\* Variation: Add a little mushroom, onion, spinach, or you can be creative with leftovers. Delicious!*

# Quiche Italienne

ALL THIS AND KOSHER TOO   BETH DAVID SISTERHOOD   MIAMI, FLORIDA

3 eggs
1¼ cups milk
2 tablespoons minced chives or scallions
½ teaspoon salt
¼ teaspoon black pepper
½ teaspoon Italian seasoning
¼ cup grated Mozzarella cheese
¼ cup grated Swiss or Cheddar cheese
⅓ cup finely grated Romano cheese
1 ripe medium tomato, thinly sliced
¼ cup finely grated Parmesan cheese
1 tablespoon butter or margarine
9- or 10-inch quiche crust (or pie crust), baked and cooled

Beat eggs slightly. Add milk, chives, salt, pepper, Italian seasoning, and the Mozzarella, Swiss, and Romano cheeses. Pour into the prebaked crust.

Place tomato slices on top of the egg mixture, then sprinkle with the Parmesan cheese and dot with butter.

Bake in a preheated 350° oven for 20 to 25 minutes. Quiche may be refrigerated and reheated the next day.

Serves 5 to 6.

# Cheese Bake

EDITORS' CHOICE

12 slices French bread
4 tablespoons butter
2 tablespoons prepared mustard
8 ounces Cheddar cheese, shredded
½ cup grated Parmesan cheese
3 eggs
3 cups milk
1 teaspoon Worcestershire sauce
½ teaspoon salt
Paprika

Combine butter and mustard, then spread the bread with this mixture. Cut each slice into quarters. In a deep, buttered 5-cup baking dish, make 3 layers *each* of bread, Cheddar cheese, and Parmesan cheese.

Beat eggs with milk, Worcestershire, and salt. Pour over bread-cheese. Sprinkle with paprika. Cover and chill at least 1 hour. May refrigerate overnight.

Bake in 350° oven for 1 hour. Serve hot.

Serves 10 to 12.

illinois world of our flavors south bend indiana the cookery cedar rapids
wa specialties of the house alexandria louisiana kitchen treats cookboo
es to noshes lewiston maine sisterhood cookbook potomac maryland p
melting pot lexington massa                    thought cookbook newton
ok norwood massachus                           ody massachusetts cc
etts in the best of tast                        e happy cooker of te
with temple beth                               a used to make f
igan all the recip                             o ask saint pau
souri deborah d                                o generation l
rry hill new je                                eating east
son new jers                                   with love s
le tinton fa                                   y the spice
ooking? al                                     onderful
k cookie                                       york the

# desserts

g brook                                        osher ki
like it cli                                    ast no
new yo                                         great r
york th                                        it vern
na hada                                        sher c
osher                                          nester
scarsc                                         what
ood ta                                         d nev
carol                                          l ohic
ount t                                         nd ok
io in t                                        nia th
ania th                                        n per
ia pen                                         penr
n wynr                                         south
charles                                        rolina
e recipe                                       0 years
nnial co                                       oks fall
nchburg                                        n good
ke it parke                                    sin from
gham alab                                      eat and en
ste berkele                                    ills califor
california fr                                  hat's cookir
flavored with                                  iego californ
lectable collec                                ease! rockvill
d connecticut fo                               passover made
earwater florida cle                           a measures and tr
ght gainesville florid                         alabustas' more fav
it in the kitchen hollywe                      s hollywood florida nil
ksonville florida what's coo                   ville florida try it you'll like
atellite beach florida our favorite recipes tallahassee florida knishes gefil
a georgia golden soup atlanta georgia the happy cooker augusta georgi
ois portal to good cooking great lakes illinois the fort sheridan and great l

# Cheese cakes

## Orange Cheesecake
THE SPORT OF COOKING  WOMEN'S AMERICAN ORT, VII  CLEVELAND, OHIO

*Crust*
1 cup flour (unsifted)
¼ cup sugar
1 tablespoon grated orange
  rind
½ cup butter
1 egg yolk
½ teaspoon vanilla

*Filling*
2½ pounds cream cheese,
  softened
1¾ cups sugar
3 tablespoons flour
1 tablespoon grated orange
  rind
¼ teaspoon salt
¼ teaspoon vanilla
5 eggs
2 egg yolks
¼ cup heavy cream
Orange sections

*Orange Glaze*
1 cup orange juice
¼ cup sugar
Dash salt
2 tablespoons cornstarch

*Crust:* Combine flour, sugar and rind. Cut in butter until mixture is crumbly. Add egg yolk and vanilla and blend thoroughly. Using an unassembled 9-inch springform pan, pat ⅓ of dough on the bottom section.

Bake in a 400° oven for 8 to 10 minutes or until golden. Cool.

Butter sides of springform pan and slip in the bottom section with the crust. Pat remaining dough 2¼ inches up sides of pan. Chill.

*Filling:* Combine cream cheese with sugar, flour, rind, salt, and vanilla. Blend well with mixer at medium speed. Add eggs and egg yolks, one at a time, blending well after each addition. Stir in cream. Pour into crust-lined pan.

Bake in a 500° oven for 8 to 10 minutes or until top of crust appears golden. Reduce heat to 225° and bake 1 hour and 20 minutes longer. Turn off heat and let stand in oven about 10 minutes. Remove from oven and cool in pan. Chill several hours or overnight.

Cover with ½ of the glaze. Dip orange sections in remaining glaze and arrange on top. Chill.

Can be decorated with orange peel rose and mint leaves.

*Glaze:* Combine the orange juice, sugar and salt. Bring to boil. Blend cornstarch and a little cold water. Stir into orange juice mixture and cook, stirring, until thickened, about 5 minutes.

Serves 12 or more.

# Splurging Cheese Cake with Strawberry Glaze

EAT AND ENJOY  PHOENIX CHAPTER OF HADASSAH  PHOENIX, ARIZONA

16 graham crackers, finely crushed
1 tablespoon flour
¼ cup melted butter
Dash cinnamon

*Filling*
16 ounces cream cheese, softened
½ pint sour cream
3 eggs
⅔ cup sugar
1 teaspoon vanilla

*Top and Glaze*
2–3 cups fresh strawberries
1 cup water
1½ tablespoons cornstarch
½ to ¾ cup sugar
Red food color, optional

Combine cracker crumbs, flour, butter, and cinnamon. Pat into an 8-inch or 9-inch springform pan.

With mixer at high speed, beat all filling ingredients for 15 minutes. Pour into crust.

Bake in a 350° oven for 40 to 50 minutes. Cool.

Cover with 1 to 2 cups whole strawberries. Pour glaze over berries. Chill 2 hours before serving.

*Glaze:* Crush 1 cup berries. Add water and cook for 2 minutes. Sieve.

Combine cornstarch and sugar. Add to hot berry mixture. Bring to a boil and cook until thick and clear, stirring constantly. Add a few drops red food color if desired. Cool to room temperature.

Serves 10 to 12.

* *Bake longer for a dry cake, shorter if you prefer creamy.*

# Pineapple Cheese Pie

BALABUSTAS — MORE FAVORITE RECIPES  B'NAI ISRAEL SISTERHOOD  GAINESVILLE, FLORIDA

8-ounce package cream cheese, softened
¼ cup sugar
1 cup heavy cream, whipped -
1½ cups crushed pineapple, drained (1-pound, 4-ounce can)
9-inch graham cracker crumb crust

Combine cream cheese and sugar and beat well. Fold in whipped cream, then pineapple. Spoon into crust and chill at least 2 hours before serving.

Serves 6 to 8.

* *Add ⅓ to ½ cup pecan halves, toasted if desired, for extra crunch.*

# Cheese Tarts

TO SERVE WITH LOVE   SISTERHOOD OF TEMPLE AVODA   FAIRLAWN, NEW JERSEY

¾ cup graham cracker
  crumbs
2 tablespoons melted butter
2 tablespoons sugar
1 can fruit pie filling
  (cherry, blueberry, or
  peach)

*Filling*
8 ounces cream cheese
¼ cup sugar
1 egg
½ teaspoon vanilla

Combine cracker crumbs, butter, and sugar. Line a miniature size cupcake pan with paper liners, then spoon 1 teaspoon crumb mixture into each cup. Press down firmly with a shot glass. Place 1 tablespoon cheese filling into each crust.

Bake in a 375° oven for 10 minutes. Cool. Cover each tart with 1 teaspoon fruit topping.

*Filling:* Combine cream cheese, sugar, egg, and vanilla. Beat until smooth.

Makes 18 tarts.

# No Crust Cream Cheese Pie

BALABUSTAS FAVORITE RECIPES   B'NAI ISRAEL SISTERHOOD   GAINESVILLE, FLORIDA

16 ounces cream cheese
3 eggs
⅔ cup sugar
½ teaspoon almond extract

*Topping*
1 pint commercial sour
  cream
3 tablespoons sugar
1 teaspoon vanilla

Combine cream cheese, 1 egg, and sugar. Beat until smooth. Add 2 more eggs and the almond extract. Beat until smooth, about 2 to 3 minutes. Pour into a well-greased 9-inch pie pan.

Bake in a 350° oven for 25 to 30 minutes. Remove from the oven when the center of the pie has risen to the level of the edge. Cool for 20 minutes. As the pie cools, the center part shrinks.

Prepare the topping by mixing together the sour cream, sugar, and vanilla.

Fill the center with sour cream topping. Return to oven and bake 10 minutes. Chill before serving.

Serves 8.

# Cream Cheese Cake

LEAVENED WITH LOVE   WASHINGTON HEBREW CONGREGATION SISTERHOOD   WASHINGTON, D.C.

*Crust*
1 cup graham cracker
   crumbs
¼ cup confectioners' sugar
¼ cup melted butter

*Filling*
1 package (3 oz.) lemon
   gelatin
1 cup hot water
16 ounces cream cheese
¾ cup sugar
1 teaspoon vanilla
1 cup heavy cream,
   whipped

Reserve up to ¼ cup graham cracker crumbs. Combine remaining crust ingredients and pat into a 9-inch or 10-inch springform pan.

Dissolve gelatin in hot water. Chill until slightly thickened. In large mixer bowl, beat cream cheese, sugar, and vanilla until fluffy. Beat in the gelatin. Remove from mixer and fold in whipped cream.

Pour into crust and top with reserved crumbs. Chill for several hours or overnight.

Serves 12.

# Cheddar Cheese Cake

FROM NOODLES TO STRUDELS   BEVERLY HILLS HADASSAH   BEVERLY HILLS, CALIFORNIA

*Crust*
1 cup flour
¼ cup sugar
½ cup butter
1 egg yolk
1 teaspoon grated lemon
   rind
¼ teaspoon vanilla

*Filling*
32 ounces cream cheese
1 cup finely grated cheddar
   cheese
¼ teaspoon vanilla
½ teaspoon grated lemon
   rind
½ teaspoon grated orange
   rind
4 whole eggs plus 2 yolks
   (can use 5 whole eggs)
1¾ cups sugar
¼ cup beer
¼ cup heavy cream

Mix ingredients for crust. Press ½ of dough into bottom of springform pan. Bake at 400° for 10 minutes. Remove from oven. Press rest of dough around edges of pan to within 1 inch of top.

Mix together cream cheese, cheddar cheese, vanilla, lemon and orange rinds. Add the whole eggs, one at a time, beating well after each addition. Add yolks and sugar. Beat well. Stir in the beer and cream carefully. Pour into crust.

Bake in a 500° oven for 8 minutes and then reduce heat to 250° and bake for another 1½ hours. Turn off oven, leaving cake in closed oven for at least 1 hour.

Serves 12 or more.

# Hot Cheese Cake

GOLDEN SOUP   AHAVATH ACHIM   ATLANTA, GEORGIA

1 cup butter, softened
½ cup sugar
2 eggs
1 teaspoon vanilla
1 cup flour
3 teaspoons baking powder
Pinch salt
¼ cup milk

*Filling*
8 ounces cream cheese
1 pound cottage cheese or
  farmers cheese
2 eggs
¼ cup sugar
Juice and rind of 1 lemon

Cream ¾ cup butter and the sugar. Add eggs and vanilla.

Mix together the flour, baking powder, and salt. Add dry ingredients alternately with milk.

Melt the remaining ¼ cup butter in a 9 x 11 pan. Spread ½ of dough in the pan. Combine ingredients for cheese filling and spread over the dough. Use the remaining dough to cover cheese; the dough may not go all the way.

Bake in a 325° oven for 40 minutes. Cool or freeze.

At serving time, add a topping of sour cream mixed with cinnamon and sugar. Then reheat at 325° until golden and bubbling, about 30 to 40 minutes more.

Serves 16.

# World's Best Chocolate Cheesecake

EDITORS' CHOICE

*Crust*
8-ounce package chocolate
  wafers, crushed
⅓ cup melted butter or
  margarine
2 tablespoons sugar
¼ teaspoon nutmeg

*Filling*
3 eggs
1 cup sugar
3 - 8-ounce packages cream
  cheese, room temperature
2 - 6-ounce packages
  semi-sweet chocolate
  chips, melted
1 teaspoon vanilla
⅛ teaspoon salt
1 cup sour cream

Preheat oven to 350°F.

Blend crust ingredients and press evenly over bottom and sides of a 9-inch springform pan. Refrigerate until needed.

With electric mixer at high speed, beat eggs with sugar until light. Beat in cream cheese until smooth. Add remaining ingredients and beat until smooth.

Pour into crust and bake 1 hour or until cheesecake is just firm when pan is shaken.

Cool cake on rack. Remove sides and cover. Refrigerate overnight.

Serves 16.

# Pies

## Grapefruit Meringue Pie
EDITORS' CHOICE

6 tablespoons cornstarch
1¼ cups sugar
¼ teaspoon salt
¼ cup cold water
2 cups fresh grapefruit
  juice
3 egg yolks
1 teaspoon grated
  grapefruit rind
1 teaspoon butter or
  margarine
1 baked 8- or 9-inch pastry
  shell

*Meringue*
3 egg whites
¼ teaspoon cream of tartar
6 tablespoons sugar

Combine cornstarch, sugar and salt in large saucepan. Stir in water and grapefruit juice. Cook over medium heat, stirring constantly, until mixture comes to a boil. Cook 5 minutes, stirring constantly. Remove from heat.

In small bowl, beat egg yolks until well mixed. Gradually stir in a small amount of hot grapefruit mixture. Then blend egg yolks into remaining hot mixture with grapefruit rind and butter. Cool for 10 minutes. Turn into pastry shell.

*Meringue:* Beat egg whites with cream of tartar until frothy. Gradually beat in sugar, 1 tablespoon at a time. Beat until stiff enough to hold sharp points. Spoon over grapefruit filling in pastry shell and spread so that it touches inner edge of crust all the way around.

Bake in a 325° oven 12 to 15 minutes until lightly browned.

Yield: 6 to 8 servings.

# Key Lime Pie
EDITOR'S CHOICE

1 egg white
1 can condensed milk
3 egg yolks, lightly beaten
¾ cup fresh lime juice
1 tablespoon grated lime
   rind
3-4 drops green food
   coloring, optional
9-inch pie shell, baked
Whipped cream, optional

Beat the egg white until stiff. Mix together milk, egg yolks, lime juice, lime rind, and food coloring. Fold in beaten egg white.

Spoon into pie shell. Chill several hours. Serve topped with whipped cream.

Serves 6 to 8.

# Lemon Glamour Pie
LOVE JEWISH STYLE   WOMEN'S ORGANIZATION OF TEMPLE ISRAEL   SOUTH ORANGE, NEW JERSEY

½ cup butter
1 cup sugar
2 eggs + 2 egg yolks
6 tablespoons lemon juice
2 teaspoons grated lemon
   peel
1 heaping teaspoon
   cornstarch
9-inch pastry shell, baked

*Meringue*
2 egg whites
4 tablespoons sugar

½ cup coconut

Cream butter and sugar in top of double boiler. Add eggs, egg yolks, lemon juice, lemon peel, and cornstarch. Mix well. Place over boiling water and cook until thick. Chill and pour into pastry shell.

Beat egg whites until stiff, gradually adding sugar. Spread on pie. Sprinkle top with coconut.

Bake in a 400° oven for 7 to 10 minutes or until golden.

Serves 6.

*For a very full meringue, add extra egg whites.*

# Pink Lemonade Pie
THE SPORT OF COOKING   WOMEN'S AMERICAN ORT, VII   CLEVELAND, OHIO

1 can (6 oz.) frozen pink
   lemonade, defrosted
1 can (14 oz.) condensed
   milk
Juice of one lemon
9-inch graham cracker
   crust, baked and cooled
Whipped cream or
   whipped topping
1 package (10 oz.) frozen
   raspberries

Combine lemonade, milk, and lemon juice. Pour into baked crust. Refrigerate for 24 hours. (Do not freeze.)

About an hour before serving, top with whipped cream. Spoon slightly defrosted raspberries and raspberry juice over each serving.

Serves 8.

# Fresh Peach Melba Pie

THE HAPPY COOKER  TEMPLE SINAI  ATLANTA, GEORGIA

1 package (10 ounces) frozen raspberries
1 tablespoon fresh lemon juice
2 tablespoons sugar
1 tablespoon brandy
1 tablespoon cornstarch
4 cups sliced fresh peaches
1 cup whipping cream
9-inch pie crust, baked

Thaw raspberries and force through a fine sieve. Place in a saucepan; add lemon juice and sugar.

Blend cornstarch with brandy and a little water. When blended, add to the raspberries. Cook mixture over medium high heat, stirring constantly until thickened.

Arrange peaches in a single layer in the prepared crust. Pour raspberry mixture over peaches and chill until ready to serve.

Top pie with whipped cream before serving.

Serves 8.

# Open Blueberry Pie

LEAVENED WITH LOVE  SISTERHOOD OF WASHINGTON HEBREW CONGREGATION  WASHINGTON, D.C.

1 quart blueberries
1 cup sugar
1 cup water
3 tablespoons cornstarch
Whipped cream
9-inch pie shell, baked

Combine sugar and water with 1 cup blueberries. Boil 8 to 10 minutes. Strain. Add cornstarch and cook over medium heat until thickened. Fold in remaining berries. Pour into pie shell. Top with whipped cream.

Serves 6 to 8.

* Strawberries may be substituted.

# Rhubarb Sour Cream Pie

PALATE TREATS  MT. ZION TEMPLE SISTERHOOD  ST. PAUL, MINNESOTA

2 cups finely cut rhubarb (uncooked)
¾ cup sugar
1 egg
1 tablespoon flour
⅛ teaspoon salt
1 cup sour cream
¼ teaspoon almond extract
9-inch pie shell, unbaked

Mix the rhubarb and sugar. Combine the egg, flour, and salt. When mixed, add the sour cream and almond extract. Mix this with the rhubarb and sugar and pour into the pie shell.

Bake in a 400° oven for 15 to 20 minutes. Then reduce heat to 350° and bake 30 to 40 minutes longer. Cool completely.

Serves 8.

# Fresh Strawberry Pie

DO IT IN THE KITCHEN   WOMEN'S AMERICAN ORT, VI   HALLANDALE, FLORIDA

1 cup 7-Up
1 cup sugar
3 tablespoons cornstarch
1 teaspoon unflavored
  gelatin
Red food coloring
2 pints fresh strawberries,
  cleaned and drained
Whipped cream
8-inch pie shell, baked

In a saucepan, combine 7-Up, sugar, cornstarch, and gelatin. Cook, stirring, until mixture thickens. Remove from heat. Add food coloring and allow to cool.

Pour a very thin layer of the cooled sauce into the pie shell. Then place all the strawberries in the pie shell. Pour remaining sauce over the strawberries and place in the refrigerator to gel — about 3 hours.

Before serving, cover the pie with whipped cream.

Serves 6.

# Strawberry Bavarian Pie

THE COOKERY   TEMPLE BETH EL SISTERHOOD   SOUTH BEND, INDIANA

2 pints fresh strawberries
¾ cup sugar
1 envelope unflavored
  gelatin
½ cup water
2 teaspoons lemon juice
1 cup heavy cream
9-inch pie shell, baked

Thinly slice 1½ pints strawberries, reserving the remainder for garnish. In a large bowl combine sliced berries and sugar; stir until sugar is dissolved.

In a saucepan, soften gelatin in water, then place over low heat and stir until gelatin dissolves. Add gelatin and lemon juice to berries.

Whip cream until stiff, and fold into strawberry mixture. Chill until mixture mounds when dropped from a spoon. Pour into baked pie shell.

Chill until set, about 4 hours. Garnish with remaining berries.

Serves 8.

# Heirloom Apple Pie

FROM DORA WITH LOVE  SISTERHOOD OF GARDEN CITY JEWISH CENTER  GARDEN CITY, NEW YORK

2 cups flour, sifted
½ teaspoon baking soda
¼ teaspoon salt
½ cup sugar
½ cup vegetable shortening
¼ cup orange juice
1 tablespoon grated orange
  rind
1 egg

*Filling*
4 pounds apples, peeled
½ cup sugar
¼ cup brown sugar
1 tablespoon flour
1 teaspoon cinnamon
1 teaspoon grated lemon
  rind
¼ cup raisins

Mix the flour, baking soda, salt, and sugar. Cut in the shortening with a pastry blender. Combine the orange juice, grated rind, and egg; beat. Blend with the other ingredients. Form into a ball, and place in refrigerator to chill while preparing the apple filling.

Slice the apples thin and combine with all the other filling ingredients. If the apples are tart, add a little more sugar.

Cut the dough into two parts. Roll out one piece on a well-floured pastry cloth and fit into a well-greased 7½ x 12 pan. Arrange the apple mixture evenly on top of the pastry.

Cover with the second piece of dough rolled out to fit. If the dough tears apart in places, just patch it up, as it won't show after it is baked. Prick the surface of the top crust for the steam to escape. You can brush the top with a little cold water before placing the pie in the oven.

Bake in a 350° oven for 1 hour or until done. Let cool and serve in squares.

Serves 12 or more.

# Apple-Yogurt Pie

IN GOOD TASTE  NATIONAL COUNCIL OF JEWISH WOMEN  CLEVELAND, OHIO

2 tablespoons flour
½ cup sugar
¾ teaspoon cinnamon
⅛ teaspoon salt
1 egg, slightly beaten
½ to 1 teaspoon vanilla
1 cup plain yogurt (or use
  vanilla yogurt and adjust
  sugar and vanilla
  accordingly)
6 apples, peeled, cored,
  and sliced
9-inch unbaked pie shell,
  chilled

*Topping*
⅓ to ½ cup flour
⅓ cup sugar
½ teaspoon cinnamon
4 tablespoons butter or
  margarine

Preheat oven to 400°.

In a large bowl, sift together flour, sugar, cinnamon, and salt. Stir in egg, vanilla, and yogurt. Fold in sliced apples. Spoon mixture into chilled pie shell.

Bake in a 400° oven for 15 minutes. Reduce oven to 350° and bake 30 minutes longer.

*Topping:* In a medium bowl, combine flour, sugar, and cinnamon. With a pastry blender or fingertips, blend in the butter until the mixture is crumbly. Sprinkle topping over pie.

Bake at 400° for 10 more minutes.

Serves 6 to 8.  Preparation time: 30 minutes.

# South's Famous Coconut Cream Pie

THE HAPPY COOKER  TEMPLE SINAI  ATLANTA, GEORGIA

⅓ cup sifted flour *or* ¼
  cup cornstarch
⅔ cup sugar
½ teaspoon salt
½ cup cold milk
3 eggs, separated
1½ cups hot milk
½ teaspoon vanilla
2 tablespoons butter
1 cup shredded coconut
3 tablespoons sugar
8- or 9-inch pie crust,
  baked

In top of double boiler, combine flour, ⅔ cup sugar, salt, and cold milk. Beat egg yolks well and stir into mixture. Gradually stir in hot milk. Cook over simmering water, stirring frequently with a wooden spoon until thickened and smooth, similar to a pudding consistency. Remove from heat; stir in vanilla, butter, and coconut. Cool slightly. Pour into pie crust.

Beat egg whites with 3 tablespoons sugar at creaming speed until they form stiff, high peaks. Spread over filling, carefully sealing meringue to pastry edges.

Bake in a 325° oven 10 to 12 minutes until lightly browned.

Serves 8.

# Own Crust Coconut Pie

IN GOOD TASTE  NATIONAL COUNCIL OF JEWISH WOMEN  CLEVELAND, OHIO

4 eggs
1¾ cups sugar
½ cup self-rising flour
2 cups milk
¼ cup butter or margarine,
  melted
1½ cups flaked coconut
1 teaspoon vanilla

Preheat oven to 350°. Grease a 10-inch pie pan.

While butter is melting, follow order of ingredients and place in a large bowl. Mix well by hand. Pour into the pie pan.

Bake in a 350° oven for 45 minutes or until top is golden. When the pie is done, turn off the oven, open oven door, and allow pie to cool gradually inside oven.

Serves 8. Preparation time: 20 minutes.


# Toasted Coconut Pecan Pie

DO IT IN THE KITCHEN  WOMEN'S AMERICAN ORT, VI  HALLANDALE, FLORIDA

3 eggs, beaten
1½ cups sugar
½ cup softened butter or
  margarine
2 teaspoons lemon juice
1 teaspoon vanilla
1 can (3½ oz.) flaked
  coconut
½ cup coarsely broken
  pecans
9-inch pie shell, unbaked

Combine eggs, sugar, butter, lemon juice, and vanilla. Stir in coconut and pecans. Pour into the pie shell.

Bake in a 350° oven for 45 minutes. Cool. Garnish with whipped cream.

Serves 6 to 8.


# Pecan Pie

THE WONDERFUL WORLD OF COOKING  BALDWIN HADASSAH  BALDWIN, NEW YORK

1 cup sugar
1 cup dark corn syrup
3 eggs, slightly beaten
2 tablespoons melted butter
  or margarine
⅛ teaspoon salt
1 teaspoon vanilla
1 cup pecan halves
9-inch pastry shell,
  unbaked

Combine sugar, corn syrup, eggs, butter, salt, and vanilla. Pour into pastry shell and decorate the top with pecan halves.

Bake in a 400° oven for 15 minutes. Reduce heat to 350° and continue baking 30 to 35 minutes longer. Pie is done when filling is set at outer edges and center is slightly soft.

Serves 8.

# Nut Pie

FAVORITE RECIPES   SISTERHOOD OF BETH ELOHIM   BROOKLYN, NEW YORK

3 eggs, separated
1 cup brown sugar
3 tablespoons flour
½ teaspoon baking powder
1 teaspoon vanilla
1 cup walnuts, chopped

Beat together egg yolks, sugar, flour, baking powder, and vanilla. Beat egg whites until stiff; fold into yolk mixture. Fold in nuts. Pour into a greased 9-inch pie plate.

Bake in a 350° oven for 20 minutes.

Serves 8.

# Peanut Butter Pie

EDITOR'S CHOICE

1 cup confectioners' sugar
½ cup + 2 tablespoons
  peanut butter
2½ cups milk
4 egg yolks, beaten
⅔ cup sugar
¼ cup cornstarch
1 rounded tablespoon flour
¼ teaspoon vanilla
Pie crust, baked and cooled

*Meringue*
4 egg whites
¼ teaspoon cream of tartar
2 tablespoons
  confectioners' sugar

Mix confectioners' sugar with ½ cup peanut butter and spread the mixture over the bottom of pie crust.

Scald milk and pour into top of double boiler. Slowly add small amount of milk to beaten egg yolks and then pour yolks into a double boiler. Mix in sugar, cornstarch, and flour. Cook until thick, stirring constantly. When done, stir in 2 tablespoons peanut butter and vanilla.

*Meringue:* Beat egg whites with cream of tartar until frothy. Gradually beat in sugar. Beat until stiff enough to hold peaks. Spoon over pie filling in shell and spread so that it touches the crust.

Bake in a 325° oven 12 to 15 minutes until lightly browned.

Yield: 6 to 8 servings.

# Golden Cups

COOK WITH TEMPLE BETH EMETH   TEMPLE BETH EMETH SISTERHOOD   ANN ARBOR, MICHIGAN

2 cups flour, sifted
¼ teaspoon salt
1 cup butter or margarine
8 ounces cream cheese,
  softened

*Filling*
2 eggs, beaten
1½ cups brown sugar,
  packed
2 tablespoons melted butter
  or margarine
Dash salt
1½ cups chopped nuts
¼ teaspoon vanilla

Sift flour and salt. Blend butter with cream cheese until no streaks appear. Blend in flour. Shape into a large ball. Refrigerate overnight.

Prepare filling by combining the filling ingredients.

When ready to bake, remove dough from refrigerator and divide into 4 parts. (Return 3 parts to refrigerator until ready to use.) Form the first section of the dough into 12 small balls. With fingers, press each ball into one section of a miniature muffin pan, leaving a slightly raised edge at top. Repeat with remaining 3 sections of dough; refrigerate all dough not being used.

Fill each muffin cup ½ to ¾ full with prepared filling. Decorate with a nut, if desired.

Bake in a 375° oven for 20 minutes or until cups are golden and filling is set. Cool 5 minutes; then remove carefully to cooling racks.

Makes 48 cups.

# Old Fashioned Buttermilk Pie

SISTERHOOD COOKBOOK   BETH JACOB SYNAGOGUE   LEWISTON, MAINE

⅔ cup sugar
3 tablespoons flour
¼ teaspoon salt
3 eggs, separated
2 cups buttermilk
¼ cup melted butter
2 teaspoons vanilla
9-inch pie shell, partially
  baked

With a fork, blend the sugar, flour, and salt. Beat the egg yolks slightly and add to dry ingredients, along with buttermilk, butter, and vanilla.

Beat the egg whites until stiff but not dry; slowly beat in yolk mixture. Pour into the pie shell.

Bake in a 425° oven for 10 minutes, then reduce heat to 325° and continue baking for 30 minutes or until a knife inserted in the center comes out clean. Cool.

Serves 8.

* *This pie is delicious served with frozen strawberries.*

# Intoxicated Sweet Potato Pie

ALWAYS IN GOOD TASTE  HAMPTON ROADS SECTION NCJW  NEWPORT NEWS, VIRGINIA

1½ cups sweet potatoes,
  mashed
¾ cup sugar
2 tablespoons melted
  butter
¼ teaspoon salt
1 egg + 2 yolks
1½ cups cream or half
  and half
2 tablespoons rum
10-inch unbaked pie shell

Meringue
2 egg whites
¼ cup plus 1 teaspoon
  sugar

Combine potatoes, sugar, and butter. Mix thoroughly. Add salt, lightly beaten whole egg and egg yolks, and cream. Add rum. Pour into the pie shell.

Bake in a 350° oven for 45 minutes or until pie is firm.

*Meringue:* Beat 2 egg whites until stiff; add ¼ cup sugar gradually; then add 1 teaspoon sugar. Spread on top of pie, and return to oven and bake until light brown.

Serves 8 to 10.

* *Be sure to spread meringue over entire filling and shell to seal completely.*

# Caribbean Fudge Pie

ONE MORE BITE  TEMPLE BETH ISRAEL SISTERHOOD  SAN DIEGO, CALIFORNIA

12-ounce package chocolate
  chips
1 tablespoon instant coffee
  powder
⅓ cup dark rum
½ cup butter
¾ cup brown sugar,
  packed
3 eggs, beaten
2 tablespoons flour
1 cup chopped macadamia
  nuts
10-inch pie shell, unbaked

Topping
1½ cups heavy cream
⅓ cup confectioners' sugar
1 tablespoon rum
½ cup chopped macadamia
  nuts

Melt chocolate over hot water and add coffee powder and rum.

In a large bowl, cream butter and sugar and add beaten eggs. Add chocolate mixture to butter mixture, blending very well. Stir in the flour and nuts. Pour into pie shell.

Bake in a 350° oven for 40 minutes. Remove from oven and cool thoroughly.

Whip cream and add confectioners' sugar and tablespoon of rum. Pile high on pie. Garnish with the rest of the nuts.

Serves 10 to 12 chocolate lovers.

# Chocolate Angel Pie
SISTERHOOD CHOICE   TEMPLE EMANUEL SISTERHOOD   EDISON, NEW JERSEY

*Meringue Shell*
**2 egg whites**
**⅛ teaspoon salt**
**⅛ teaspoon cream of tartar**
**½ cup sugar, sifted**
**½ cup finely chopped pecans**
**½ teaspoon vanilla**

*Chocolate Filling*
**1 package (4 oz.) German's sweet chocolate**
**3 tablespoons water**
**1 teaspoon vanilla**
**1 cup heavy cream, whipped**

Beat the egg whites with the salt and cream of tartar until foamy. Add the sugar slowly, beating until very stiff peaks are formed. Fold in the nuts and ½ teaspoon vanilla. Spread into a greased 8-inch pie pan and build up sides ½ inch above the pan.

Bake in a preheated 300° oven for 50 to 55 minutes. Cool.

Combine chocolate and water and melt over low heat (or in a double boiler), stirring constantly. Cool until thick. Add 1 teaspoon vanilla. Fold in the whipped cream and pile into the meringue shell. Chill for 2 hours.

Serves 6.

# Chocolate Velvet Cream Pie
TRY IT, YOU'LL LIKE IT   JACKSONVILLE JEWISH CENTER   JACKSONVILLE, FLORIDA

*Crust*
**1½ cups finely crushed chocolate wafers**
**⅓ cup butter or margarine**

*Filling*
**8 ounces cream cheese, softened**
**½ cup sugar**
**1 teaspoon vanilla**
**2 eggs, separated**
**6-ounce package semi-sweet chocolate chips, melted**
**1 cup heavy cream, whipped**
**¾ cup chopped pecans**

Combine chocolate wafers with butter. Press into bottom of a 9-inch springform pan.

Bake in 325° oven for 10 minutes.

Combine cream cheese, ¼ cup sugar, and vanilla, mixing until well blended. Stir in beaten egg yolks and melted chocolate. Beat egg whites until soft peaks form. Gradually beat in ¼ cup sugar. Fold into chocolate mixture. Fold in whipped cream and chopped pecans. Pour into crust. Freeze.

Serve frozen, decorated with whipped cream.

Makes 8 to 10 generous servings.

# Flaky Pie Crust

EDITOR'S CHOICE

2 cups flour
¼ teaspoon baking powder
½ teaspoon salt
⅔ cup vegetable shortening
Few drops vinegar
⅓ cup ice cold water

Sift flour, baking powder, and salt into a mixing bowl. With a pastry blender or two knives cut in shortening until mixture resembles coarse cornmeal.

Mix vinegar with water and sprinkle over flour, a tablespoon at a time, mixing. Work quickly and with a light touch. Do not knead. Wrap and chill.

Divide dough in two balls, one slightly larger than the other (for the bottom crust). Roll out on floured pastry cloth.

Pastry for 9-inch two-crust pie.

* *Hint: When sprinkling water over the flour, save about a spoonful to mix with the flour that invariably stays at the bottom of the bowl after you've made the ball.*

# No-Roll Pastry for One-Crust Pie

BALABUSTAS — MORE FAVORITE RECIPES   B'NAI ISRAEL SISTERHOOD   GAINESVILLE, FLORIDA

1½ cups flour
1½ teaspoons sugar
1 teaspoon salt
½ cup oil
2 tablespoons milk

Sift flour, sugar, and salt directly into pie pan.

Combine oil and milk. Whip with fork and pour into middle of flour. Mix. Press to the sides and bottom of the pan. Prick for an unfilled crust.

Bake in a 425° oven for 12 to 15 minutes.

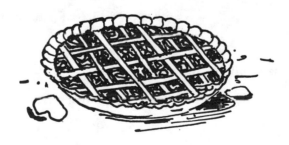

# Cakes

## Honey Cake

EAT AND ENJOY   HADASSAH CHAPTER   PHOENIX, ARIZONA

3½ cups sifted flour
¼ teaspoon salt
1½ teaspoons baking
  powder
1 teaspoon baking soda
½ teaspoon cinnamon
½ teaspoon nutmeg
⅛ teaspoon powdered
  cloves
½ teaspoon ginger
4 eggs
¾ cup sugar
4 tablespoons salad oil
2 cups dark honey
½ cup brewed coffee
1½ cups nuts

Sift together flour, salt, baking powder, and soda. Stir in the cinnamon, nutmeg, cloves and ginger. Beat the eggs and gradually add the sugar. Beat until thick and light in color.

Beat in oil, honey, and coffee. Stir in the flour mixture and the nuts.

Oil two 9-inch loaf pans or one 11 x 16 x 4 pan and line with foil.

Bake in a 325° oven for 1½ hours for the large pan (or 50 minutes for the 2 smaller pans) until browned and tester comes out clean. Cool on a rack before removing from pans.

Serves 12 to 16.

# Honey Chiffon Cake

SALT AND PEPPER TO TASTE   SISTERHOOD, CONGREGATION ANSHEI ISRAEL   TUCSON, ARIZONA

3 eggs, separated
½ teaspoon cream of tartar
3½ cups flour
1 cup sugar
2½ teaspoons baking
  powder
1 teaspoon baking soda
½ teaspoon salt
1 teaspoon cinnamon
¼ teaspoon cloves
¼ teaspoon ginger
¼ cup oil
1 pound honey
1½ cups strong coffee,
  warm
1 cup blanched almonds

Beat egg whites with cream of tartar until stiff. Set aside.

Sift together flour, sugar, baking powder, baking soda, salt, cinnamon, cloves, and ginger. Make well in center; add yolks, oil, honey, and coffee. Beat well. Fold in egg whites and mix gently until well blended. Add almonds. Pour into a large ungreased tube pan.

Bake in a 350° oven for about 1 hour.

Serves 12 to 14.

# Fritzie's Famous Pound Cake

DO IT IN THE KITCHEN   WOMEN'S AMERICAN ORT, VI   HALLANDALE, FLORIDA

3-ounce package cream
  cheese
½ cup unsalted butter
1 cup sugar
2 eggs
1½ cups self-rising flour
½ cup milk
1 teaspoon vanilla or lemon
  extract

Mix cream cheese, butter, and sugar. Add the eggs, one at a time, beating after each. Then add the flour alternately with the milk, finishing with the flour. Blend in the flavoring. Pour into a greased and floured 9 x 9 or small Bundt pan.

Bake in a 350° oven for 45 to 60 minutes.

Serves 8 to 10.

# Nut Pound Cake

TRY IT ... YOU'LL LIKE IT   TEMPLE BETH EL   CHAPPAQUA, NEW YORK

3 cups flour
1¾ cups sugar
2 teaspoons baking powder
1½ teaspoons salt
1 cup soft shortening
¾ cup milk
2 teaspoons vanilla
4 eggs
1 cup chopped walnuts

In large mixer bowl, combine the flour, sugar, baking powder, salt, shortening, milk, and vanilla; beat until well-blended. Add eggs, 2 at a time, beating after each addition. Fold in walnuts. Pour into 2 greased loaf pans.

Bake in a 375° oven for about 60 minutes.

# Sour Cream Pound Cake

OUR FAVORITE RECIPES  BETH SHALOM SISTERHOOD  SATELLITE BEACH, FLORIDA

1 cup butter
3 cups sugar
6 eggs, separated
1 teaspoon vanilla
1 teaspoon grated lemon
  rind
3 cups flour
¼ teaspoon baking powder
¼ teaspoon baking soda
1 cup sour cream

Cream butter and sugar. Add yolks, one at a time, beating well after each. Add vanilla and lemon rind.

Sift flour with baking powder and baking soda. Add dry ingredients to batter alternately with sour cream. Mix well.

Beat egg whites until stiff but not dry. Fold egg whites into batter. Pour into a large, greased tube pan.

Bake in a 300° oven for 2 hours. Invert pan to cool.

Serves 14 to 16.

# Butterscotch Pound Cake

THE HAPPY COOKER  TEMPLE SINAI SISTERHOOD  ATLANTA, GEORGIA

6-ounce package
  butterscotch morsels
2 tablespoons instant coffee
  powder
¼ cup water
1 cup butter
1½ cups sugar
3 cups flour
½ teaspoon soda
¼ teaspoon salt
¾ cup buttermilk
4 eggs

Melt butterscotch morsels in double boiler with coffee and water. Cream butter and sugar. Blend in butterscotch mixture.

Combine flour, soda, and salt. Add to creamed mixture alternately with buttermilk.

Add eggs one at a time, beating at medium speed after each addition. Pour into a greased Bundt pan.

Bake in a 350° oven for 55 to 60 minutes. Cool 10 minutes before removing from pan.

Serves 12 to 14.

# Banana Cake

THE COOKERY  TEMPLE BETH EL SISTERHOOD  SOUTH BEND, INDIANA

1 cup butter
3 cups sugar
4 eggs, separated
2 cups bananas (heaping)
2 teaspoons vanilla
3 cups cake flour
Pinch salt
2 teaspoons soda
½ cup sour cream or milk

Cream butter. Add sugar and beat until smooth. Add egg yolks, bananas, and vanilla.

Sift flour, salt, and soda together. Add alternately with sour cream.

Beat egg whites and fold into mixture. Pour into an 11 x 17 pan.

Bake in a 400° oven for 8 minutes, then reduce heat to 325° and bake about 1 hour longer. Test for doneness.

Serves 20.

* Easy and very good.

# Banana Split Cake

THE HAPPY COOKER  TEMPLE SINAI  ATLANTA, GEORGIA

1 cup butter or margarine
1½ cups sugar
4 eggs
½ cup mashed banana
½ cup sour cream
½ cup milk
1 teaspoon vanilla
3 cups all-purpose flour
2 teaspoons baking powder
1 teaspoon salt
¼ teaspoon baking soda
½ cup strawberry
  preserves
Few drops red food
  coloring
½ cup instant cocoa
  powder
Confectioners' sugar

In large mixer bowl, cream butter and sugar. Add eggs, one at a time, beating well after each addition.

Combine bananas, sour cream, milk, and vanilla. Combine flour, baking powder, salt, and baking soda; add to creamed mixture alternately with banana mixture, beating well after each addition.

Remove 1 cup of the batter and mix it with strawberry preserves and red food coloring. Combine another 1 cup of batter with cocoa powder. Spoon half of the remaining (plain) batter into a well-greased and floured 10-inch fluted tube pan. Cover with strawberry batter, then the remaining plain batter, then the chocolate batter.

Bake in a 350° oven for 1 hour 10 minutes or until done. Cool in pan 10 minutes; remove from pan. Cool on rack.

Sift confectioners' sugar over cooled cake. Serve with ice cream topped with additional strawberry preserves, if desired.

Serves 12 to 14.

# Jamaican Cake

THE STUFFED BAGEL  HADASSAH CHAPTER  COLUMBIA, SOUTH CAROLINA

3 cups flour
1 teaspoon baking soda
1 teaspoon cinnamon
2 cups sugar
1 teaspoon salt
1½ cups oil
1 can (8 oz.) crushed
   pineapple with juice
1½ teaspoons vanilla
3 eggs
2 cups ripe banana, diced

Combine flour, baking soda, cinnamon, sugar, and salt and *mix by hand*. Do not use mixer.

Add the oil, pineapple, vanilla, eggs, and banana. Blend well by hand. Pour into a greased tube or Bundt pan.

Bake in a 325° oven for 1½ hours.

Serves 12 to 14.

*Cover the cut up bananas with the pineapple to keep them from turning dark.*

# Pineapple Upside Down Cake

ABIGAIL SERVES  UNITED ORDER OF TRUE SISTERS  ALBANY, NEW YORK

¼ cup butter
¾ cup brown sugar
Canned pineapple (sliced
   or diced)
Walnuts
Maraschino cherries

*Cake*
¼ cup shortening
½ cup sugar
1 egg
1 cup self-rising cake flour
⅓ cup milk
½ teaspoon vanilla

Melt butter in 2-inch high round cake pan. Cover with brown sugar, spread evenly. Arrange pineapple slices in a pattern over the sugar, placing walnuts, and then cherries, where desired to form a design.

Cream shortening and sugar. Add egg and beat. Add flour alternately with milk, beating after each addition. Add vanilla. Pour into pan over fruit.

Bake in a 350° oven for 40 to 50 minutes.

Serves 8 to 10.

*For a pareve cake, substitute the pineapple or other fruit juice for the milk in the recipe.*

# Caramel Pineapple Roll Cake

TO SERVE WITH LOVE   SISTERHOOD OF BETH EL   LEVITTOWN, PENNSYLVANIA

1 can (#2) crushed
  pineapple
½ cup brown sugar
4 large eggs, separated
¾ cup sugar
1 teaspoon vanilla
½ teaspoon grated lemon
  rind
¾ cup cake flour
1 teaspoon baking powder
1 teaspoon salt
Confectioners' sugar

*Icing*
4 tablespoons butter
4 ounces cream cheese
1 cup confectioners' sugar
1 tablespoon pineapple
  juice
1 teaspoon vanilla

Butter a 10 x 15 jelly roll pan. Drain the pineapple, reserving 1 tablespoon of the juice for the icing. Spread the pineapple over the pan and sprinkle with brown sugar.

In large mixing bowl, beat egg whites until foamy; slowly add ½ cup sugar. Continue beating until stiff.

In a small bowl, beat the yolks with remaining ¼ cup sugar until thick. Fold yolk mixture into stiffened whites and add vanilla and lemon rind.

Sift the flour, baking powder, and salt; sprinkle over all and gently fold in. Spread batter over the pineapple mixture in pan.

Bake in a 375° oven for 18 to 20 minutes. Turn upside down on a damp towel sprinkled with confectioners' sugar. Roll up and cool in the towel. Remove towel as soon as it cools. (May be frozen at this point.)

*Icing:* Cream butter and cream cheese; gradually add sugar, reserved pineapple juice, and vanilla. Mix until smooth. Frost cake roll, running fork tines in wavy lines to pattern it. May decorate cake with violets and leaves.

Serves 10 to 12.


# Date and Nut Cake

BALABUSTAS — MORE FAVORITE RECIPES   B'NAI ISRAEL SISTERHOOD   GAINESVILLE, FLORIDA

1 cup chopped nuts
1 cup seedless raisins
1 cup chopped dates
½ cup boiling water
1¼ cups flour
¾ cup sugar
1 teaspoon baking soda
¼ cup butter
1 egg, beaten
1 teaspoon vanilla

Combine nuts, raisins, dates, and boiling water. In another bowl, combine flour, sugar, baking soda, butter, egg and vanilla. Combine two mixtures. Place in a heavily greased pound cake pan (loaf pan).

Bake in a 350° oven for 50 to 60 minutes or until toothpick comes out clean. May be frozen.

Serve plain or with whipped cream.

Makes 8 servings.

# Pumpkin Walnut Cake

THE MELTING POT   JEWISH COMMUNITY CENTER   AMHERST, MASSACHUSETTS

3 cups flour, sifted
2 teaspoons baking powder
2 teaspoons baking soda
1 teaspoon salt
3½ teaspoons cinnamon
4 large eggs
2 cups sugar
1½ cups corn oil
1 can (1 lb.) pumpkin
1 cup coarsely chopped
 walnuts

Sift together flour, baking powder, baking soda, salt, and cinnamon. Set aside.

In a large bowl, with mixer at high speed, beat eggs until yolks and whites are combined. Gradually add sugar until mixture is thick and lemon colored. Add oil.

With mixer at low speed, blend in dry ingredients alternately with pumpkin, beginning and ending with dry ingredients. Beat until smooth. Add walnuts. Pour into lightly greased tube or Bundt pan.

Bake in a 350° oven for 1 hour to 1 hour 10 minutes. Cool 15 minutes.

Serves 12 to 14.

* This cake is very moist and freezes well. Enjoyed by all testers.

# Carrot Fig Loaf

ROCHESTER HADASSAH COOKBOOK   ROCHESTER CHAPTER OF HADASSAH   ROCHESTER, NEW YORK

1½ cups all-purpose flour
1 cup sugar
1 teaspoon baking powder
1 teaspoon baking soda
¼ teaspoon cinnamon
¼ teaspoon salt
⅔ cup oil
2 eggs
1 teaspoon vanilla extract
1 cup raw carrots, finely
 shredded
¾ cup snipped dried figs
½ cup flaked coconut

*Lemon Glaze*
1 teaspoon grated lemon
 rind
1 cup confectioners' sugar
Hot water

Place dry ingredients into large bowl of electric mixer. Add oil, eggs, and vanilla. Mix for 2 minutes. Stir in carrots, figs, and coconut. Pour into a greased and lightly floured 5 x 9 loaf pan.

Bake in a 350° oven for 1 hour or until done. Cool for 5 minutes. Remove from pan.

Combine lemon rind and confectioners' sugar. Add enough hot water to make a stiff frosting. Glaze and cool.

Serves 10 to 12.

# Carrot Cake
BALABUSTAS — MORE FAVORITE RECIPES  B'NAI ISRAEL SISTERHOOD  GAINESVILLE, FLORIDA

2 cups sugar
2 cups flour
2 teaspoons baking soda
1 teaspoon salt
2 teaspoons cinnamon
1 cup oil
4 eggs
3 cups grated carrots
1 teaspoon vanilla

*Frosting*
½ cup butter or margarine
8 ounces cream cheese
1 box confectioners' sugar
1 cup chopped pecans
1 teaspoon vanilla

In a large mixer bowl combine sugar, flour, soda, salt, and cinnamon. Add oil; then eggs, one at a time, beating well after each addition. Add carrots and vanilla; beat well. Pour into a greased and floured 10-inch tube pan.

Bake in a 350° oven for 55 minutes or until done.

*Frosting:* Cream butter and cream cheese. Add sugar, pecans, and vanilla. Beat until smooth. Does not need to be refrigerated.

Serves 12 to 14.


# Pecan Roll
TO SERVE WITH LOVE  SISTERHOOD OF BETH EL  LEVITTOWN, PENNSYLVANIA

6 eggs, separated
½ cup sugar
1 cup finely chopped
  pecans
¼ teaspoon salt
1 cup heavy cream
3 teaspoons Cointreau
2 teaspoons confectioners'
  sugar

Beat egg yolks and sugar until light and thick. Fold in the pecans.

Beat egg whites with salt until firm peaks are formed. Fold into yolk mixture.

Grease a jelly roll pan. Cover with greased waxed paper and pour in batter.

Bake in a 350° oven for 15 minutes or until cake breaks away from sides of pan. Turn cake out on waxed paper that has been sprinkled with confectioners' sugar. Immediately peel off top paper carefully and roll up cake loosely to prevent splitting. Cool.

Whip cream, add Cointreau and confectioners' sugar. Unroll cake and spread with whipped cream; roll up again.

Serves 8 to 10.

# Orange-Butter Cake

THE PREPARED TABLE  SOLOMON SCHECTER DAY SCHOOL  HUNTINGDON VALLEY, PENNSYLVANIA

¾ cup unsalted butter,
  room temperature
1 cup sugar
1 tablespoon grated orange
  rind
1 teaspoon vanilla
3 eggs
1 cup orange marmalade
3 cups flour (may be 2
  cups white flour and 1
  cup whole wheat flour)
1½ tablespoons baking soda
1 teaspoon salt
½ cup orange juice
½ cup evaporated milk
1 cup chopped nuts (or
  plumped raisins)

Cream butter; add sugar, orange rind, and vanilla, and beat until mixture is light and fluffy. Add eggs, one at a time, beating well after each addition. Add marmalade.

Combine flour, baking soda, and salt; add to creamed mixture alternately with combined orange juice and milk. Stir in nuts. Pour into a well-greased 10-inch tube pan.

Bake in a 350° oven for 55 to 60 minutes. Cool 10 minutes before removing from pan.

Serves 10 to 12.

* This is a rich and moist cake that freezes well.


# Orange Streusel Cake

THE WONDERFUL WORLD OF COOKING  BALDWIN HADASSAH  BALDWIN, NEW YORK

½ cup butter
1 cup brown sugar, firmly
  packed
2 eggs, well beaten
2 cups all-purpose flour
3 teaspoons baking powder
Pinch salt
½ cup orange juice
½ cup milk
2 teaspoons vanilla
1 teaspoon grated orange
  rind

*Streusel Topping*
⅓ cup brown sugar
⅓ cup flour
3 tablespoons butter
1 teaspoon sugar
1 teaspoon grated orange
  rind

Cream butter and sugar. Add eggs. Sift flour, baking powder, and salt together and add to the creamed mixture. Beat well. Add orange juice and milk. Blend in vanilla and grated orange rind. Pour into a greased 9 x 9 pan and sprinkle with topping.

Bake in a 350° oven for 45 minutes.

*Streusel topping:* Combine all ingredients and mix until crumbly in texture.

Serves about 16.

*"I keep trying to lose weight, but it keeps finding me."

# Gateau Grand Marnier

THE SPORT OF COOKING   WOMEN'S AMERICAN ORT, VII   CLEVELAND, OHIO

1 cup butter
1 cup sugar
3 eggs, separated
1 teaspoon Grand Marnier
2 cups flour, sifted
1 teaspoon baking powder
1 teaspoon baking soda
1 cup sour cream
Grated rind of 1 orange
½ cup chopped nuts

*Sauce*
½ cup sugar
¼ cup orange juice
⅓ cup Grand Marnier
Sliced almonds

Cream butter and 1 cup sugar until light and fluffy. Add egg yolks, one at a time, and continue beating. Add 1 teaspoon Grand Marnier.

Beat egg whites until stiff and set aside.

Sift together flour, baking powder, and baking soda. Add to batter alternately with sour cream, beginning and ending with dry ingredients. Stir in grated rind and nuts. Fold in egg whites. Pour into a greased 9-inch or 10-inch angel food pan.

Bake in a 350° oven for 50 to 55 minutes or until cake tests done.

Combine ½ cup sugar, orange juice, and ⅓ cup Grand Marnier. Spoon over cake as soon as it comes from the oven.

Let cake cool, remove from the pan, and turn right side up. Stud cake with sliced almonds to decorate.

Serves 12. Freezes very well.

*\* Hint: Take off a scant ¼ cup flour and mix it with the nuts and grated rind; add to the batter with the last of the dry ingredients. This prevents the nuts and rind from sticking to the bottom.*

# Orange Kiss-Me Cake
IN GOOD TASTE   JEWISH COMMUNITY CENTER   STATEN ISLAND, NEW YORK

6 ounces frozen orange
  juice concentrate, thawed
2 cups flour
1 cup sugar
1 teaspoon soda
1 teaspoon salt
½ cup shortening
½ cup milk
2 eggs
Coconut

Grease and flour a 9 x 13 pan.

In large mixer bowl, combine 4½ ounces juice with all other ingredients except coconut. Blend at low speed for 30 seconds, then beat 3 minutes at medium speed. Pour into pan.

Bake in a 350° oven for 45 minutes.

While cake is still warm, poke holes in the top with a fork and pour remaining juice over it. When cool, cover the cake with coconut.

Serves 12 to 14.

*This cake is very quick and easy to make.*

# Apple Dapple Cake
KITCHEN KNISHES   AGUDATH SHALOM CONGREGATION   LYNCHBURG, VIRGINIA

2 cups sugar
1½ cups oil
3 eggs
3 cups flour
1 teaspoon baking soda
1 teaspoon baking powder
1 teaspoon salt
1 teaspoon cinnamon
1 teaspoon nutmeg
2 teaspoons vanilla
3 cups chopped firm
  apples
1 cup pitted dates
1 cup chopped pecans
1 small can shredded
  coconut

Combine sugar and oil in large bowl. Stir to mix well. Add eggs, one at a time, beating well after each addition.

Combine flour, soda, baking powder, salt, cinnamon and nutmeg, and stir into oil mixture. Add vanilla, apples, dates, pecans and coconut. Mix well. Spoon batter into a greased 10-inch tube pan.

Bake in a 325° oven for 1½ hours or until cake tests done.

Serves 14 to 16.

# Fresh Apple Bran Cake

MENU MAGIC  BETH ISRAEL SISTERHOOD  FLINT, MICHIGAN

1½ cups flour, sifted
2 teaspoons baking soda
1 teaspoon cinnamon
1 teaspoon nutmeg
½ teaspoon salt
½ cup butter or margarine
1½ cups sugar
2 eggs, well beaten
4 cups apples, pared and
  finely cut
1 cup whole bran cereal

Sift together flour, baking soda, cinnamon, nutmeg, and salt.

In a large bowl, cream butter and sugar, beating until fluffy. Add eggs and blend well. Stir in apples, cereal, and dry ingredients. Spread in a well-greased 9 x 13 pan.

Bake in a 350° oven for 40 minutes or until done. When cool, spread with a fluffy frosting and cut into squares.

Makes 24 two-inch squares.

* This cake is very moist and also very good unfrosted.


# Gentleman's Party Cake

BALABUSTAS — MORE FAVORITE RECIPES  B'NAI ISRAEL SISTERHOOD  GAINESVILLE, FLORIDA

4 eggs, separated
1 heaping cup sugar
7 or 8 ounces ground
  almonds
1 tablespoon potato starch
1 teaspoon almond extract
⅓ cup liqueur, brandy, or
  sherry
⅓ cup water
⅓ cup sugar
Whipped cream, slivered
  almonds, chocolate
  sprinkles (optional)

Beat egg yolks with sugar until mixture turns white. Add almonds, potato starch, and almond extract. Fold in stiffly beaten egg whites. Pour into a 9 x 9 pan, buttered and lined with greased waxed-paper.

Bake in a 350° oven for 45 minutes. Allow to cool in pan.

Pierce all over with a toothpick. Combine the liqueur, water, and ⅓ cup sugar; pour over cake. Allow the mixture to soak in well for about 1 hour.

Turn the cake out onto a platter and garnish with 1 cup whipped cream, slivered almonds, and sprinkles of chocolate.

Serves 9 to 12.

# Poppyseed Cake
EDITORS' CHOICE

3 cups all-purpose flour
  (not sifted)
2 cups sugar
1½ teaspoons baking soda
½ teaspoon salt
4 eggs
1½ cups oil
1 large can evaporated milk
1 teaspoon vanilla
1 can poppyseed filling
1 cup chopped nuts

Combine flour, sugar, baking soda, salt, eggs, oil, milk, and vanilla in a large mixing bowl. Beat on low speed until blended and then on medium speed until well blended. Add poppyseed filling and nuts. Beat for 2 minutes at medium speed. Put mixture in an ungreased 10-inch tube pan.

Bake in a 350° oven for about 1 hour and 15 minutes. Let cake stand for about an hour or until cool.

Shake powdered sugar over top for decoration.

Serves 12 to 14.

# Heath Bar Cake
IN GOOD TASTE   NATIONAL COUNCIL OF JEWISH WOMEN   CLEVELAND, OHIO

2 cups flour, sifted
1 cup brown sugar
½ cup sugar
½ cup butter
1 cup chopped nuts
1 cup chocolate chips
7 Heath bars, chopped
1 teaspoon baking soda
1 cup buttermilk
1 egg, beaten
1 teaspoon vanilla
¼ cup chopped nuts
2 Heath bars, chopped

Preheat oven to 350°. Grease and flour a 9 x 13 pan.

Mix flour and sugars in large bowl. Cut in butter until as fine as cornmeal. Reserve ½ cup for topping.

Add 1 cup nuts, chocolate chips, and 7 Heath bars to remaining flour mixture. Add baking soda to buttermilk and stir into mixture. Add egg and vanilla; stir well. Pour mixture into prepared pan.

Add ¼ cup nuts and 2 Heath bars to reserved crumb mixture. Sprinkle over batter.

Bake for 35 minutes. Cool before serving.

Serves 8 to 10. Preparation time: 30 minutes.

# Queen of Sheba Cake

ENJOY, ENJOY  SISTERHOOD OF TEMPLE ISRAEL OF GREAT NECK  GREAT NECK, NEW YORK

4 ounces semi-sweet
  chocolate
2 tablespoons dark rum
½ cup butter
⅔ cup sugar
3 eggs, separated
Pinch salt
1–2 tablespoons sugar
¾ cup cake flour, sifted
⅓ cup pulverized almonds
¼ teaspoon almond extract

*Icing*
3 ounces semi-sweet
  chocolate
1½ tablespoons dark rum
6 tablespoons butter,
  softened
Whole blanched almonds

Butter and flour an 8-inch cake pan.

Melt chocolate; add rum. In large mixing bowl, cream butter and sugar until fluffy. Beat in egg yolks until well blended.

In separate bowl, beat egg whites with a pinch of salt until soft peaks form. Sprinkle with 1 to 2 tablespoons granulated sugar, and beat until stiff peaks form.

With rubber spatula, blend chocolate into creamed mixture, then stir in flour, almonds, and almond extract. Immediately stir in ⅓ of the beaten egg whites to lighten the batter. Lightly fold in remaining egg whites. Turn batter into cake pan and push up to rim with spatula.

Bake in middle level of oven at 350° for 20 to 25 minutes. Cake is done when puffed and a toothpick inserted comes out clean. (Center of cake will be slightly wet when toothpick is inserted.) Cool 10 minutes. Run knife around edge. Reverse on a rack and cool thoroughly, about 1 hour.

*Icing:* Melt chocolate, add rum. Add 1 tablespoon butter at a time. Beat until smooth. Beat over cold water to spreading consistency.

Spread icing on cake, then make a design around the edge with the whole almonds.

Serves 8 to 10.

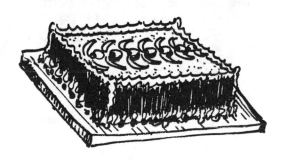

# Chocolate Zucchini Cake

SISTERHOOD COOKERY  SISTERHOOD OF BROOKLYN HEIGHTS SYNAGOGUE  BROOKLYN, NEW YORK

2½ cups all-purpose flour, unsifted
½ cup cocoa, unsweetened
2½ teaspoons baking powder
1½ teaspoons baking soda
1 teaspoon salt
1 teaspoon cinnamon
¾ cup butter or margarine, softened
2 cups sugar (1½ cups if using sweetened cocoa)
3 eggs
2 teaspoons vanilla
2 teaspoons orange juice
2 cups unpeeled zucchini, coarsely shredded
½ cup milk
1 cup chopped walnuts

Combine flour, cocoa, baking powder, soda, salt, and cinnamon; set aside.

Cream the butter and sugar until they are smoothly blended. Add eggs, one at a time, beating well after each addition. With a spoon, stir in the vanilla, orange juice, and zucchini.

Stir the dry ingredients and the milk alternately into the zucchini mixture, including the nuts with the last addition. Pour batter into a greased and floured 10-inch tube or Bundt pan.

Bake in a 350° oven for about 1 hour. Cool in pan for 15 minutes, then turn out on wire rack to cool thoroughly.

Serves 12 to 14.

# Fifty Dollar Fudge Cake

MENU MAGIC  BETH ISRAEL SISTERHOOD  FLINT, MICHIGAN

4 tablespoons butter
2 cups sugar
2 eggs, separated
4 squares unsweetened chocolate, melted
2 cups flour, sifted
2 teaspoons baking powder
1½ cups milk
2 teaspoons vanilla
½ pound nutmeats, broken

In a large mixing bowl, cream butter and sugar until light and fluffy. Add egg yolks, one at a time, mixing well after each addition. Add the cooled melted chocolate, mixing well.

Sift flour and baking powder together and add alternately to the batter with milk and vanilla. Mix in nuts.

Beat egg whites until stiff; fold into batter. Turn into a 9 x 13 Pyrex baking dish.

Bake in a 325° oven for 1 hour (for a metal pan, bake in a 350° oven). When cool, spread with chocolate frosting.

Makes about 24 pieces.

*This cake is heavy and chocolate-y!*

# Waldorf Astoria Chocolate Cake

ROCHESTER HADASSAH COOKBOOK   HADASSAH CHAPTER   ROCHESTER, NEW YORK

½ cup butter
2 cups sugar
2 eggs
2 cups all-purpose flour
½ teaspoon salt
2 teaspoons baking powder
1½ cups milk
4 squares baking chocolate, melted
1 teaspoon vanilla
1 cup chopped pecans

*Frosting*
1½ squares chocolate
¼ cup butter
¼ teaspoon salt
1⅓ cups confectioners' sugar
1 egg, well beaten
1 cup coarsely chopped pecans
1 teaspoon vanilla
1 tablespoon lemon juice

Cream butter and sugar; add eggs, one at a time. Sift flour, salt, and baking powder together and add alternately with milk to creamed mixture, beginning and ending with flour. Add melted chocolate and vanilla. Stir in pecans. Pour into greased tube pan.

Bake in a 350° oven for 50 minutes or until done. Do not invert pan after removing from oven. Remove cake from pan after it cools. Frost, but do not cut for 24 hours.

*Frosting:* Melt chocolate with butter; add salt. Add remaining ingredients except for nuts, beating until of spreading consistency. Stir in nuts.

Serves 12 to 14.

# Milky Way Cake

PIDDLAR IN THE KITCHEN   AUGUSTA HADASSAH   AUGUSTA, GEORGIA

6 Milky Way candy bars
1 cup butter
2 cups sugar
4 eggs
2½ cups flour, sifted
½ teaspoon baking soda
1¼ cups buttermilk
1 teaspoon vanilla
1 cup chopped nuts

Melt candy and ½ cup butter in a saucepan over very low heat. Set aside.

Beat sugar and remaining ½ cup butter in a medium-sized bowl until fluffy. Add eggs, one at a time, beating well after each addition. Add flour and baking soda alternately with buttermilk; stir until smooth. Add candy mixture, mixing well. Stir in vanilla and nuts. Pour into greased and floured Bundt pan.

Bake in a 350° oven for 1 hour and 15 to 25 minutes (test with toothpick). Cool in pan on wire rack for 10 minutes. Remove from pan.

Serves 12 to 16.

# Bittersweet Chocolate Cake

FROM DORA WITH LOVE   SISTERHOOD OF GARDEN CITY JEWISH CENTER   GARDEN CITY, NEW YORK

½ cup butter
2 cups brown sugar
3 eggs, separated
2 cups flour
1½ teaspoons baking
  powder
1 teaspoon baking soda
½ cup milk
½ cup sour cream
2 squares bitter chocolate,
  shaved or grated
3 cups sweet cream
5 tablespoons chocolate
  syrup

Cream butter and sugar until thick and well blended. Add egg yolks and beat until thick and creamy. Combine the flour, baking powder, and baking soda and add to the egg mixture alternately with the milk and sour cream, which have been mixed together.

Stir the chocolate into the batter and mix well. Beat the egg whites until stiff but not too dry and fold into the batter. Pour into two greased 9-inch layer cake pans.

Bake in a 350° oven for 40 minutes. Let cool on wire racks.

After the cake is cold, slice each layer in half, making four layers. Whip the cream and fold in the chocolate syrup. Assemble the cake, spreading whipped cream between the layers and over the top and sides. Decorate with shaved chocolate on top.

Serves 10 to 12.

*Everyone goes off their diet when this cake is served.*

# Chocolate Pudding Cake

THE COOK'S BOOK   SUBURBAN JEWISH COMMUNITY CENTER   HAVERTOWN, PENNSYLVANIA

1 cup flour
¾ cup sugar
2 teaspoons baking powder
½ teaspoon salt
2½ tablespoons cocoa
½ cup milk
1 teaspoon vanilla
1 tablespoon melted butter
½ cup pecans, chopped
Whipped cream, optional

*Chocolate Syrup*
½ cup sugar
½ cup light brown sugar,
  packed
2 tablespoons cocoa
1 cup boiling water

Combine flour, sugar, baking powder, salt, and cocoa. Add milk, vanilla, and butter. Blend thoroughly. Stir in nuts. Turn batter into an 8 x 8 or 9 x 9 pan.

Combine syrup ingredients. Pour carefully over top of batter.

Bake in a 350° oven 40 to 45 minutes. Cool.

When cool, turn upside down on a serving plate, letting chocolate syrup from the bottom of the pan run over the cake. Serve with whipped cream.

Makes 8 servings.

# Mahogany Sour Cream Cake

ESSEN 'N FRESSEN  CONGREGATION BETH CHAIM  EAST WINDSOR, NEW JERSEY

3 squares unsweetened
  chocolate
½ cup water
2 cups cake flour
1 teaspoon salt
1 teaspoon baking soda
1½ teaspoons baking
  powder
⅔ cup butter
1 cup sugar
⅔ cup light brown sugar
3 eggs
2 teaspoons vanilla
1 cup sour cream

Combine chocolate and water. Heat until chocolate melts; cool.

Sift together flour, salt, soda, and baking powder.

In a large bowl, cream butter and sugars. Add eggs, one at a time, beating well after each addition. Blend in vanilla. Add sour cream to chocolate. Add alternately with flour to egg mixture. Pour into two greased and floured 9-inch cake pans.

Bake in a 350° oven for 35 to 40 minutes.

Serves 12 to 14.

*Top with whipped cream or assemble with your favorite frosting.*

# Chocolate Chip Raisin Cake

ROCHESTER HADASSAH COOKBOOK  ROCHESTER HADASSAH  ROCHESTER, NEW YORK

1 cup hot water
1 teaspoon baking soda
1 cup raisins
1 cup butter or margarine
1 cup sugar
3 eggs
⅛ to ¼ cup orange juice
1 teaspoon vanilla
3 cups flour
2 teaspoons baking powder
Pinch salt
6-ounce package chocolate
  chips

Mix hot water, baking soda, and raisins; refrigerate 1 hour. Cream butter and sugar; add eggs. Drain raisins, reserving the liquid. Add "raisin liquid" to orange juice and vanilla.

Sift together flour, baking powder, and salt; add raisins and chocolate chips. Add to creamed mixture, then add liquid. Pour into a well-greased tube pan.

Bake in a 350° oven for 1 hour.

Serves 12 to 14.

# Chocolate Roll

THE MELTING POT   JEWISH COMMUNITY OF AMHERST   AMHERST, MASSACHUSETTS

6 eggs, separated
½ cup sugar
6 ounces semi-sweet
  chocolate chips
3 tablespoons strong coffee
1 teaspoon vanilla
Cocoa
Confectioners' sugar
1½ cups heavy cream,
  whipped and sweetened

Butter an 11 x 14 x 1 pan; line it with waxed paper and butter the paper.

Beat the egg yolks until light and lemon colored; gradually beat in the sugar. Melt the chocolate with coffee in the top of a double boiler. Let cool slightly, then add to egg yolks. Beat well. Beat in vanilla.

Beat the egg whites until stiff enough to form peaks (but do not beat dry). Fold into the chocolate mixture. Pour batter into the prepared pan, spreading evenly.

Bake in a 350° oven for 15 minutes or until a knife inserted into the center comes out clean. Remove from the oven; cover with a damp towel and let stand for about 20 minutes.

Tear an 18-inch length of waxed paper and place on work area; sprinkle with cocoa and confectioners' sugar. Run a spatula around the edges of the cake and invert on the waxed paper; it should turn out easily. Carefully remove the paper on which it was baked.

Spread the cake with sweetened whipped cream. Then, by lifting the edge of the waxed paper under the cake, get the long end of the cake to fold inward; this starts the cake rolling. Continue lifting the waxed paper and roll up the cake gently and quickly onto a large platter.

Serves 8 to 10.

*Uses no flour – excellent for Passover.*

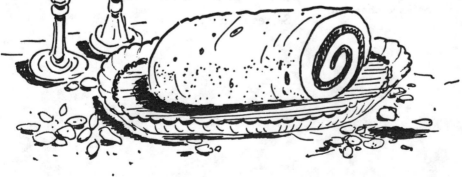

# Bavarian Gugelhuph

SEASON TO TASTE   TEMPLE B'NAI ISRAEL SISTERHOOD   PARKERSBURG, WEST VIRGINIA

2 cups all-purpose flour, sifted
1 tablespoon double-acting baking powder
1 teaspoon salt
⅔ cup unsalted butter or margarine
1 cup sugar
4 eggs
½ cup milk
1 teaspoon vanilla
24 blanched almonds, slivered
2 squares semi-sweet chocolate, grated

Sift together flour, baking powder, and salt.

Cream butter; add sugar gradually, creaming well. Add eggs, one at a time, beating well after each.

Combine milk and vanilla. Add alternately with dry ingredients; blend thoroughly after each addition with mixer at low speed.

Arrange almonds over the bottom of a well-greased and lightly floured 10-inch tube pan (fluted or standard). Carefully spoon ⅓ of the batter into the pan and spread evenly over nuts. Cover with ½ the grated chocolate. Spoon in another ⅓ of the batter, spreading carefully. Cover with remaining grated chocolate. Top with the final ⅓ of the batter.

Bake in a 350° oven for 55 to 65 minutes. Let cool in pan for 15 minutes. Turn out on rack. Sprinkle with sugar.

Serves 12 to 14.

* The fluted pan gives the gugelhuph a characteristic design.

# Chocolate Applesauce Cupcakes

DEBORAH DISHES   MID-MISSOURI—DEBORAH CHAPTER OF HADASSAH   COLUMBIA, MISSOURI

½ cup shortening
1 cup sugar
1 egg (unbeaten)
1 cup applesauce
1½ cups flour, sifted
⅓ cup cocoa
1½ teaspoons apple pie spice (cloves, nutmeg, allspice, and cinnamon)
1 teaspoon baking soda
1 teaspoon water
Frosting
Coconut

Cream shortening and sugar. Add egg and beat well. Put the applesauce through a sieve; add. Sift flour, cocoa, and spices three times; add. Dissolve baking soda in water; add and mix well. Pour into greased muffin pans, ½ full.

Bake in a 350° oven 25 to 30 minutes. Decorate with favorite frosting and top with coconut.

Makes 16.

# Coconut Bars

EDITORS' CHOICE

1 yellow cake, 9 x 13
1½ cups sugar
½ cup baking cocoa
1 cup water
8 ounces grated coconut
(buy at bakery or health
food store)

Bake favorite yellow cake or marble cake. Cool on rack while in pan. Cut into 1½ x 4½ inch pieces (approximately). Do not remove from pan. Cover with wrap and freeze.

Combine sugar, cocoa, and water in a saucepan. Boil gently for 5 minutes. Pour in a shallow container, such as a pie pan. Pour coconut into a second shallow pan.

Remove cake from freezer and remove pieces from pan. With left hand, take one frozen cake piece and dip in hot chocolate mixture; coat on all sides. Place in coconut pan.

Use right hand to coat all sides with coconut. Remove and place on waxed-paper lined cookie sheet. Do not let bars touch each other.

Keep left hand for chocolate mixture and right hand for coconut or you will have a terrible mess!

Return to freezer. When frozen, the bars may be packaged in plastic bags.

Makes 18 bars.

*This is a popular Cleveland specialty. You'll see why when you taste them. (Since these are messy to make, it's a good idea to make a double recipe.)*

# Miniature Black Bottom Cupcakes

TO SERVE WITH LOVE   SISTERHOOD OF BETH EL   LEVITTOWN, PENNSYLVANIA

8-ounce package cream
  cheese
1 egg
⅓ cup sugar
⅛ teaspoon salt
1 small package chocolate
  chips
1½ cups sifted flour
1 cup sugar
¼ cup dark Hershey's
  cocoa powder
½ teaspoon salt
1 teaspoon baking soda
1 cup water
½ cup oil
1 tablespoon vinegar
1 teaspoon vanilla

In small mixing bowl, beat together the cream cheese, egg, ⅓ cup sugar, and ⅛ teaspoon salt. Add chocolate chips and mix in by hand.

In large mixing bowl, blend all the remaining ingredients and beat well.

Line small muffin tins with cupcake papers. Place 1 tablespoon chocolate mixture in each cup, then top with 1 teaspoon of the cream cheese mixture.

Bake in a 350° oven for 25 minutes.

Makes 48.

# Malt Shake Cupcakes

WHAT'S COOKING IN ORT   WOMEN'S AMERICAN ORT CHAPTER   JACKSONVILLE, FLORIDA

½ cup butter, softened
½ cup boiling water
1 cup instant chocolate
  malted milk powder
1 cup flour
½ cup sugar
1½ teaspoons baking
  powder
½ teaspoon salt
2 eggs, slightly beaten
1 teaspoon vanilla
¼ cup chopped walnuts

*Icing*
1 cup confectioners' sugar
2 tablespoons hot water
½ teaspoon vanilla
Dash salt
8 maraschino cherries, cut
  in halves

Preheat oven to 375°.

Melt butter in water in a 1-quart jar. Add ¾ cup malted milk powder, flour, sugar, baking powder, salt, eggs, and vanilla. Cover tightly. Shake about 10 times. Stir lightly. Shake vigorously until well-blended.

Fill muffin pans (with paper liners) ⅔ full. Sprinkle with the remaining ¼ cup malt powder and walnuts. Bake for 20 to 25 minutes. Cool.

Mix all icing ingredients, except cherries, together and drizzle over cooled cupcakes. Top each with a cherry half.

Yield: 12 to 16 cupcakes.

*No bowl or beaters; just shake in jar! Unusual and simple method.*

# One Egg Cupcakes

COUNCIL'S COOK-IN  NATIONAL COUNCIL OF JEWISH WOMEN  BAYSHORE, NEW JERSEY

1¼ cups cake flour
¾ cup sugar
2 teaspoons baking powder
½ teaspoon salt
⅓ cup shortening
½ cup milk
1 teaspoon vanilla or lemon
  extract
1 medium egg (unbeaten)

Heat oven to 375°.

Combine flour, sugar, baking powder, and salt. Add shortening; mix. Add milk and vanilla. Beat 1½ minutes. Add egg; beat about 1½ minutes.

Turn into cupcake pans either greased or cupped with papers. Fill pans about ½ full. Bake for about 20 minutes or until a testing toothpick comes out clean from center of cupcake.

Makes 12.

# Pear Sherry Cupcakes

GOLDEN SOUP  AHAVATH ACHIM SISTERHOOD  ATLANTA, GEORGIA

¾ cup shortening
1½ cups brown sugar
2 eggs
3 cups flour, sifted
¾ teaspoon soda
¾ teaspoon salt
1½ teaspoons cinnamon
½ cup sherry (or other
  wine or juice)
¼ cup water
2 cups diced fresh pears
  (unpeeled)
½ cup pecans, chopped

Cream shortening and sugar well. Add eggs and beat well.

Sift flour with soda, salt, and cinnamon. Add to creamed mixture alternately with sherry and water, beating well after each addition. Stir in the pears and pecans. Fill paper baking cups ⅔ full.

Bake in a 350° oven for 25 to 30 minutes.

Makes 2 dozen cupcakes.

*Tasty as is, but may be frosted.*

# Date and Nut Cupcakes — Miniatures

QUICK AND EASY COOKBOOK  MAIN LINE REFORM TEMPLE SISTERHOOD  WYNNEWOOD, PENNSYLVANIA

1 cup chopped walnuts
1 cup chopped dates
1 cup coconut (4 oz. can)
½ cup sugar
3 eggs, beaten

Combine all ingredients and turn into greased miniature cupcake pans.

Bake in a 350° oven for 25 to 30 minutes.

Makes 24.

*These are good for Passover — no flour needed. Also, they freeze well.*

# Vanilla Icing
COOK'S CHOICE   BRANDEIS UNIVERSITY NATIONAL WOMEN'S COMMITTEE   WESTCHESTER SHORE, NEW YORK

4 tablespoons butter
2 cups confectioners'
 sugar, sifted
3 tablespoons milk (about)
1 teaspoon vanilla
Dash salt

Cream butter; add ½ to ⅓ cup sugar gradually, blending after each addition. Add remaining sugar alternately with milk, beating after each addition until right consistency to spread. Add vanilla and salt.

Covers sides and top of a 9-inch cake.

# Strawberry Icing
EAT AND ENJOY   HADASSAH CHAPTER   PHOENIX, ARIZONA

1 egg white
1 cup sugar
1 cup fresh strawberries,
 crushed

Place all ingredients in mixer bowl and beat for 15 minutes. Decorate with whole berries. This icing is very good on a sponge cake. Decorate with whole berries.

Covers a 10-inch sponge cake.

* If you use frozen berries, they must be well drained before using.

# Dora's Favorite Chocolate Icing

FROM DORA WITH LOVE  SISTERHOOD OF GARDEN CITY JEWISH CENTER  GARDEN CITY, NEW YORK

1 egg
3 tablespoons shortening
  (butter, margarine, or
  vegetable)
3 tablespoons cocoa
3 tablespoons fine sugar
1 teaspoon flavoring

In a small mixing bowl, beat egg; add all the other ingredients and beat until the consistency of whipped cream.

This recipe is delicious on chocolate cake. Decorate with pecan or walnut halves or chopped nuts.

*Variation:* By adding 1 teaspoon of instant coffee you can change the chocolate icing to mocha icing.

*Notes:* If the icing should separate a little while in the mixing bowl, add an extra teaspoon of sugar. Sometimes one egg is larger than another, therefore you need more sugar, or half sugar and half cocoa.

Covers top of average cake.

* *"This has been a family favorite for over forty years. Double the recipe for a layer cake. Or double the recipe and freeze half."*

# Fabulous Fudge Frosting

EDITOR'S CHOICE

3 cups sugar
3 tablespoons light corn
  syrup
1 cup milk
4 squares unsweetened
  chocolate
⅓ cup butter
1 teaspoon vanilla

Put sugar, corn syrup, milk, and chocolate into large saucepan. Cook over medium heat, stirring until sugar is dissolved. Continue cooking until small amount of mixture forms a very soft ball in very cold water (232° F. on a candy thermometer), stirring occasionally to prevent scorching.

Remove from heat, add butter without stirring, and cool until lukewarm, about 1 hour. Add vanilla and beat until frosting is creamy.

Covers a 9-inch layer cake.

* *If frosting stiffens before spreading is completed, add ½ to 2 teaspoons water and beat until smooth.*

# Luscious Lemon Frosting

COOK'S CHOICE  BRANDEIS UNIVERSITY NATIONAL WOMEN'S COMMITTEE  WESTCHESTER SHORE, NEW YORK

3 tablespoons butter
1 tablespoon grated orange
  rind
3 cups confectioners'
  sugar, sifted
2 tablespoons lemon juice
1 tablespoon water
Dash salt

Cream butter; add orange rind and cream well. Add about ¾ cup sugar gradually, blending after each addition. Combine lemon juice and water; add to creamed mixture alternately with remaining sugar until right consistency to spread. Add salt and beat smooth.

Covers two 9-inch layers or 3 dozen cupcakes.

# Strudels & tortes

## Strudel
THE CENTER TABLE COOKBOOK   MISKAN TEFILA   NEWTON, MASSACHUSETTS

*Filling*
**2 oranges**
**½ lemon**
**1 package seedless raisins**
**½ cup sugar**
**3 tablespoons jam**
**3 tablespoons matzo meal
  or bread crumbs**
**1½ cups broken walnuts**

*Dough*
**2½ cups flour**
**¼ cup sugar**
**½ teaspoon baking powder**
**1 egg**
**½ cup oil**
**½ cup lukewarm water**
**Additional oil**
**Sugar and cinnamon**
**Confectioners' sugar**

Grind oranges, lemon, and raisins. Add sugar, jam, and matzo meal; mix thoroughly. Set aside.

Sift flour, sugar, and baking powder into a mixing bowl. Add the egg, ½ cup oil, and water; beat with fork into a soft dough. Divide into four pieces. Knead each piece lightly on floured board. Roll out into a very thin sheet; brush with oil and sprinkle with cinnamon and sugar.

Spread one-fourth of the filling over the lower third of the dough. Sprinkle the entire sheet with one-fourth of the nuts, and roll up like a jelly roll, starting from lower edge. Place on a well-oiled cookie sheet. Prepare remaining three pieces of dough in the same manner. Brush tops with oil and sprinkle with sugar and cinnamon. With kitchen scissors or sharp knife, cut through top layer of dough every 1½ inches.

Bake in 400° oven for 15 minutes, then reduce heat to 375° and continue baking about 30 minutes more or until well browned.

Remove from oven and sprinkle with confectioners' sugar. Cut each piece through and remove carefully from pan with a knife. Do not stack while warm.

Makes about 60 pieces.

\* *"This is my grandmother's recipe, which was originally printed in the 1950 edition of the cookbook. It is my mom's Rosh Hashana specialty."*

# Ice Cream Strudel

COOK ALONG WITH US  SISTERHOOD OF TEMPLE BETH SHALOM  PEABODY, MASSACHUSETTS

1 pint vanilla ice cream
1 cup butter
2 cups flour
Melted butter
Cinnamon-sugar mixture

*Filling*
12 ounces apricot jam
1 tablespoon lemon juice
1 cup chopped nuts
½ cup raisins
½ cup coconut
¼ cup chopped maraschino
  cherries

Combine softened ice cream, 1 cup butter, and flour and mix thoroughly. Roll in ball and refrigerate overnight. (Or place in freezer for 1 hour.)

Combine all ingredients for filling.

Allow ice cream mixture to return to room temperature. Divide into 3 parts. Roll each part out on a floured surface. Spread with filling and roll up like a jelly roll. Brush with melted butter, then sprinkle with cinnamon-sugar mixture. Place on a greased cookie sheet.

Bake in a 350° oven for 35 minutes.

Makes about 36 pieces.

*This recipe makes a minimal amount of filling. You may want to increase – even double – the amounts of nuts, raisins, coconut, and cherries.*

# Easy Strudel

FLAVORED WITH LOVE  ADAT ARI EL SISTERHOOD  NORTH HOLLYWOOD, CALIFORNIA

1 cup butter, room
  temperature
2 cups flour
1 cup sour cream, room
  temperature
1 jar (16 oz.) apricot
  preserves
1 package coconut (6 oz.)
3½ ounces nuts, chopped
Confectioners' sugar

Cut butter into flour with pastry blender. Add sour cream and mix thoroughly. Divide dough into three equal sections. Wrap each in plastic wrap and refrigerate for several hours or overnight.

To assemble, remove one section of dough from refrigerator and roll out on a floured board into a rectangle about ⅛-inch thick. Spread with thin layer of preserves. Sprinkle with ⅓ of the nuts and coconut. Roll up, jelly-roll style, and place on ungreased cookie sheet. Roll and fill remaining sections of dough the same way.

Bake in a 350° oven for 45 minutes or until nicely browned. Cool and slice. Sprinkle with confectioners' sugar before serving.

Makes about 30 pieces.

# Baklava

FAVORITE RECIPES   TEMPLE EMANU-EL SISTERHOOD   ROCHESTER, NEW YORK

2 cups walnuts
1 cup almonds
3 slices bread, toasted
⅓ cup sesame seeds
¼ cup sugar
1 teaspoon cinnamon
1 package filo leaves
½ cup oil (approximately)

*Syrup*
3 cups sugar
3 cups water
½ cup honey
½ teaspoon lemon juice

Grind together walnuts, almonds, bread, and sesame seeds. Add sugar and cinnamon and mix well. Remove filo leaves from package and cover with a damp towel.

Brush a 9 x 13 pan with oil. Lay 2 filo leaves in pan, one on top of the other, and brush with oil; then another 2 filo leaves, and brush with oil. Sprinkle some of the nut mixture on top. Continue pattern of 2 leaves, oil, 2 leaves, oil, and nut mixture until you have finished. Cut lengthwise in 1½-inch strips, then cut diagonally to make a diamond-shaped pastry.

Bake in a 350° oven for 30 minutes or until golden brown. Pour hot syrup over pastry before removing from oven. Allow to cool overnight.

*Syrup:* Combine sugar and water. Bring to a boil and continue cooking for 15 minutes until slightly thick. While still boiling, add honey and lemon juice.

Makes about 40 pieces.

# Almond Torte

FROM GENERATION TO GENERATION   B'NAI AMOONA SISTERHOOD   ST. LOUIS, MISSOURI

7 eggs, separated
1 cup sugar
1 tablespoon grated lemon rind
2 cups finely chopped almonds

Beat egg whites until stiff; add sugar slowly. Beat egg yolks until light. Fold beaten whites into yolks. Add lemon rind and almonds. Pour into a 9-inch springform pan.

Bake in a 350° oven for about 1 hour.

This cake may be filled and frosted or you may dust the top with sifted confectioners' sugar.

Serves 10 to 12.

# Chocolate Almond Torte

THE HAPPY COOKER OF TEMPLE SHALOM   TEMPLE SHALOM   WEST NEWTON, MASSACHUSETTS

8 eggs, separated
1 cup sugar
4 ounces semi-sweet
  chocolate, melted
½ cup fine bread crumbs
1 cup finely chopped
  almonds
1 cup apricot jam

*Frosting*
6 egg yolks
⅓ cup very strong coffee
¾ cup sugar
¾ cup unsalted butter

Beat egg whites until stiff. Set aside. Grease three 8-inch layer pans (or one 10 x 15 baking sheet), line with waxed paper, and grease again.

Beat the egg yolks and sugar together until thick and lemon colored. Stir in the melted chocolate, bread crumbs, and almonds, and then fold in the egg whites. Spread into baking pans.

Bake in a 325° oven for 30 minutes or until cake springs back when pressed lightly. Turn out of pans and remove paper at once. Cool.

Put the layers together with apricot jam. (If cake has been baked on a sheet, cut it into 3 strips and put together with jam.)

In top of double boiler, beat together the 6 egg yolks, coffee, and sugar. Cook, stirring constantly, until mixture thickens, about 5 minutes. Cool to room temperature. Add butter, bit by bit, and beat until thick enough to spread. Cover sides and top with frosting.

Serves 12 to 14.

# Easy Way Chocolate Torte

TRY IT ... YOU'LL LIKE IT   TEMPLE BETH EL SISTERHOOD   CHAPPAQUA, NEW YORK

1 frozen pound cake
8 ounces semi-sweet
  chocolate
¼ cup strong coffee
2 tablespoons Cognac
1½ cups heavy cream

Cut cake in 6 horizontal layers while it is still partially frozen.

Melt chocolate in coffee in the top of a double boiler over hot, not boiling water. When smooth, add Cognac and allow to cool.

Whip cream and fold into chocolate mixture. Place in freezer for about 20 minutes or until mixture starts to set.

Fill layers and ice all over with whipped cream mixture. Refrigerate. Slice thin when ready to serve.

Serves 8 to 10.

*This is a wonderful dessert to have in the freezer.*

# Viennese Torte

TO SERVE WITH LOVE   SISTERHOOD OF CONGREGATION BETH EL   LEVITTOWN, PENNSYLVANIA

½ cup butter or margarine
6-ounce package chocolate
  chips
1 teaspoon instant coffee in
  ¼ cup water *or* 1 ounce
  Cointreau or white rum
4 egg yolks
2 tablespoons
  confectioners' sugar,
  sifted
1 teaspoon vanilla
1 pound cake
1 cup apricot preserves
2 tablespoons water
Pistachio nuts, ground
  (optional)

Melt butter and chocolate with coffee in double boiler. Cool. Beat egg yolks with sugar and vanilla; add to chocolate. Chill 45 minutes.

Cut cake into 6 slices lengthwise (cuts easier if chilled). Trim evenly.

Melt apricot preserves with 2 tablespoons water. Strain.

Spread each slice of cake with apricot, then with chocolate mixture. When all slices are covered, assemble and ice sides and top with chocolate mixture. If desired, decorate with ground pistachio nuts. Refrigerate. Slice thin to serve.

Serves 8 to 10.

Note: Quantities are designed for a Sara Lee frozen cake. If using a home-baked pound cake that is larger, double the recipe.

*Flavor improves if cake is made the day before it is served.*

# Cherry Chocolate Torte à la Liesl

DO IT IN THE KITCHEN   WOMEN'S AMERICAN ORT, VI   HALLANDALE, FLORIDA

3 ounces unsalted butter
  (¾ stick), room
  temperature
⅔ cup sugar
6 large eggs, separated
6 ounces ground almonds
6 ounces semi-sweet
  chocolate chips, melted in
  double boiler
1 can pitted black cherries,
  drained well
Confectioners' sugar

Mix butter, sugar, and egg yolks well. Add the almonds. Stir lightly. Pour in melted chocolate and stir. Beat egg whites until very stiff and fold into mixture.

Pour into a well-greased and floured 12-inch springform pan. Drop the cherries into the cake.

Bake in a 300° oven for 1½ hours. Sprinkle with confectioners' sugar when cool. Serve with whipped cream, if desired.

Serves 10 to 12.

*This recipe may be used during Passover. It can be doubled (use a 9 x 13 pan). Freezes well.*

# Cherry Torte

2 cups sour cherries
  (1 can)
1¼ cups sugar
1 cup flour
1 teaspoon cinnamon
1 teaspoon soda
¼ teaspoon salt
1 egg white, well beaten
1 tablespoon melted butter
1½ cups walnuts (large
  pieces)

*Cherry Sauce*
1 cup juice from cherries
1 tablespoon cornstarch
½ cup sugar
1 tablespoon butter
Pinch salt

Drain cherries, reserving the liquid.

Sift dry ingredients together. Fold in beaten egg white and butter, then cherries and nuts. Pour into an 8 x 8 torte pan.

Bake in a 350° oven for 45 to 60 minutes. Cut into squares. Serve with cherry sauce and whipped cream.

*Cherry Sauce:* Heat cherry juice (from can) in a small saucepan. Mix the sugar, cornstarch, and salt together with 2 tablespoons of cherry juice to make a smooth paste. Then stir vigorously into rest of hot cherry juice. When thickened, add butter. For a thicker sauce, use 1½ tablespoons cornstarch.

Serves 9 to 12.

# Fruit Torte

FOOD FOR THOUGHT   TEMPLE EMUNAH SISTERHOOD   LEXINGTON, MASSACHUSETTS

½ cup butter
1 cup sugar
1 cup flour, sifted
1 teaspoon baking powder
Dash salt
2 eggs
1 pint blueberries, sliced
  peaches, or sliced apples
Cinnamon-sugar mixture

Cream butter and sugar. Add flour, baking powder, salt, and eggs. Mix well. Pour into a greased 9-inch springform pan. Cover entire surface of cake with a fruit of your choice. (Be sure to drain the fruit first. It should be dry.) Sprinkle cinnamon and sugar mixture over the top.

Bake in a 350° oven for 1 hour. Can be frozen.

Serves 10 to 12.

*Good served warm with vanilla ice cream.*

# Raspberry Torte Cake

KITCHEN TREATS COOKBOOK   ALEXANDRIA TEMPLE SISTERHOOD   ALEXANDRIA, LOUISIANA

1 cup butter
1½ cups sugar
5 eggs, separated
2 tablespoons milk
3 teaspoons vanilla
¾ teaspoon salt
½ teaspoon baking powder
2 cups sifted flour
1½ cups seedless raspberry
  preserves (or black
  raspberry)
1 cup coconut
2 cups sour cream

Cream butter; add ½ cup sugar and cream well. Blend in egg yolks, milk, 1½ teaspoons vanilla, ½ teaspoon salt, and baking powder; beat well. Stir in flour.

Grease three 9-inch cake pans. Spread batter in pans, then spread preserves over each layer to within 1 inch of edge.

Beat egg whites and ¼ teaspoon salt until mounds form. Slowly add 1 cup sugar, beating well. Beat until stiff peaks form, then fold in coconut and 1½ teaspoons vanilla. Spread over preserves.

Bake in a 350° oven for 35 to 40 minutes. Cool 15 minutes, remove from pans and cool completely.

Assemble cake, spreading sour cream between layers; garnish with more preserves and chill several more hours before serving.

Serves 12 to 14.

# Jaffe Torte

IN THE BEST OF TASTE   CONGREGATION BETH EL   SUDBURY, MASSACHUSETTS

2 cups flour
1 teaspoon baking powder
1 teaspoon baking soda
⅔ cup ground walnuts
1 cup butter
1 cup sugar
3 eggs, separated
¾ cup sour cream
2 tablespoons *each* grated
  orange rind and grated
  lemon rind
⅛ teaspoon salt

*Glaze*
¾ cup sugar
2 tablespoons orange juice
2 tablespoons lemon juice

Mix flour, baking powder, and baking soda. Stir a few spoons of the dry ingredients into the walnuts.

Cream butter and sugar; then beat in egg yolks one at a time. Add dry ingredients alternately with sour cream. Add the nuts and stir in the grated rinds.

Beat egg whites with salt till they hold a peak. Fold them into the batter. Pour into a 9-inch springform pan that has been buttered and coated with fine bread crumbs or flour.

Bake in a 350° oven for 1 hour or until done.

*Glaze* (prepare a few minutes before cake is done): Mix sugar and juices in small pot and bring to boil, stirring to dissolve sugar. When cake is out of the oven, prick the top quickly with a small, sharp knife and brush the hot glaze over the hot cake till it is absorbed. Let the cake cool in the pan.

Serves 12 to 14.

# Baba Au Rhum

COOK'S CHOICE   BRANDEIS UNIVERSITY NATIONAL WOMEN'S COMMITTEE   WESTCHESTER SHORE, NEW YORK

5 eggs, separated
1 cup sugar
1 box Zweiback or Holland
  Rusk, crushed

*Syrup*
2 tablespoons sugar
½ cup water
½ cup rum

Beat egg yolks and sugar. Add crushed Zweiback. Fold in stiffly beaten egg whites. Turn into a well-greased 9- or 10-inch ring mold.

Bake in a 350° oven for 25 to 30 minutes. Remove from pan to cool. Allow to dry. Return to pan in which cake was baked.

*Syrup:* Dissolve sugar in water; heat. Add rum. Pour over cake. Soak thoroughly with this mixture.

Unmold and serve. Fill center with fruit or whipped cream.

Serves 8 to 10.

# Chocolate Puffs

THE WONDERFUL WORLD OF COOKING   BALDWIN HADASSAH   BALDWIN, NEW YORK

¼ cup butter
½ cup water
½ cup flour, sifted
2 eggs

*Cocoa Whipped Cream*
1 cup heavy cream
2 tablespoons cocoa
4 tablespoons
  confectioners' sugar
⅛ teaspoon salt
1 teaspoon vanilla

*Hot Fudge Sauce*
3 ounces (3 squares)
  unsweetened chocolate
5 tablespoons butter
3 cups confectioners'
  sugar, sifted
1 cup evaporated milk
1 tablespoon vanilla

Combine butter and water in saucepan and bring to boil. Reduce heat and add flour all at once, stirring rapidly. Cook and stir for about 2 minutes until mixture thickens and leaves sides of pan. Remove from heat. Add eggs, one at a time, beating well after each addition. Beat until mixture is satiny and breaks off when spoon is raised.

Drop mixture from a teaspoon onto an ungreased baking sheet, shaping into 1-inch mounds.

Bake in a 425° oven for 20 minutes or until golden brown.

When puffs are cool, cut off tops, fill with Cocoa Whipped Cream, and replace tops. Serve with Hot Fudge Sauce.

*Cocoa Whipped Cream:* Combine all ingredients in a small bowl. Chill 1 hour, then beat until cream holds its shape.

*Hot Fudge Sauce:* Melt chocolate and butter in a saucepan. Remove from heat. Add sugar alternately with evaporated milk, blending well after each addition. Bring to boil over medium heat, stirring constantly. Cook and stir until mixture becomes thick and creamy, about 8 minutes. Add vanilla.

Makes about 36.

# Coffee cakes & brunch

## Babka

EDITOR'S CHOICE

5-6 cups all-purpose flour
2 packages yeast
¼ cup warm water
1 cup + 2 tablespoons
  sugar
1 teaspoon salt
3 eggs, slightly beaten
½ cup butter or margarine
¼ cup butter or margarine,
  melted
1 cup milk
¼ cup salad oil

*Filling*
¾ cup sugar
1 - 3 teaspoons cinnamon
½ cup raisins
½ cup broken walnuts

Put 3 cups flour into a large bowl. Make a well in the center. Dissolve yeast in warm water mixed with 2 tablespoons sugar; pour into well. Add 1 cup sugar and the salt.

Melt ½ cup butter in the milk. Remove from heat and mix in the oil. Beat the butter mixture into the flour a little at a time, alternating with the eggs. Then beat in 2 or 3 cups more flour until mixture is no longer sticky.

Knead on floured surface for 8 to 10 minutes until smooth. Oil a large bowl. Roll the dough in the bowl until all surfaces are covered with oil. Cover with tea towel and let rise in a warm place until double in size. Punch down and turn out on the counter. Cover and let rest 10 minutes.

Divide into 4 parts. Roll each part into a rectangle ⅛-inch thick. Brush with melted butter. Combine topping ingredients and sprinkle on rectangles. Roll each like a jelly roll and place around a greased tube pan. Cover and let rise again until double. Brush top with 1 egg yolk beaten with 1 tablespoon water for crispy crust. For soft crust brush with butter.

Bake in a 325° oven for 1 hour. Remove from pan and let cool on rack.

*For a less rich babka, reduce sugar and butter/oil to about three-fourths the quantities given.*

# Favorite Sour Cream Coffee Cake

IN GOOD TASTE  NATIONAL COUNCIL OF JEWISH WOMEN  CLEVELAND, OHIO

½ cup walnuts, finely
  chopped
1½ cups sugar
1 teaspoon cinnamon
½ cup butter or margarine,
  softened
1 cup sour cream
2 eggs
1 teaspoon vanilla
2 cups flour
1 teaspoon baking powder
1 teaspoon baking soda

Preheat oven to 350°. Grease a 9-inch tube pan.

In a small bowl, combine nuts, ½ cup sugar, and cinnamon. Set aside.

In a large bowl, with mixer at medium speed, cream 1 cup sugar with butter until light and fluffy. Add sour cream, eggs, vanilla, flour, baking powder, and soda and beat at low speed until blended, then beat at medium speed for 3 minutes. Keep scraping bowl with rubber spatula.

Spread half of batter in the pan and sprinkle with half of nut mixture. Cover with remaining batter and sprinkle with remaining nut mixture.

Bake for 60 to 65 minutes or until cake pulls away from the pan. Cool in pan on wire rack for 10 minutes. Loosen edges and invert from pan onto rack to cool slightly.

Serve warm. If serving later, cool completely and wrap.

Serves 10 to 12. Preparation time: 20 minutes.

* Variation: Apple Sour Cream Coffee Cake

Prepare as above. Spread ½ batter in pan. Layer as follows: ⅓ nut mixture, 1 medium apple that has been peeled and thinly sliced, another ⅓ nut mixture, remaining batter, remaining nut mixture. Bake for 65 to 70 minutes. Cool completely in pan on wire rack.

# Cream Cheese Coffee Cake

BALABUSTAS: MORE FAVORITE RECIPES   B'NAI ISRAEL SISTERHOOD   GAINESVILLE, FLORIDA

½ cup butter
8 ounces cream cheese
1¼ cups sugar
2 eggs
2 cups flour
1 teaspoon baking powder
½ teaspoon baking soda
¼ teaspoon salt
¼ cup milk
1 teaspoon vanilla

*Topping*
⅓ cup brown sugar
2 tablespoons butter
⅓ cup flour
½ teaspoon cinnamon

Cream butter and cream cheese. Gradually add sugar, continuing to beat. Add eggs, one at a time, beating after each addition. Combine flour, baking powder, baking soda, and salt and add alternately with milk. Add vanilla. Spread in a greased 9 x 13 cake pan.

Combine topping ingredients until crumbly, and sprinkle over cake top.

Bake in a 350° oven for about 35 to 40 minutes. Cut into squares when cool.

Serves 16.

# Pecan Rolls

COOK ALONG WITH US   SISTERHOOD OF TEMPLE BETH SHALOM   PEABODY, MASSACHUSETTS

1 small yeast cake (or 1 pkg. dry yeast)
½ cup sour cream
1 cup butter
2 tablespoons sugar
1 egg, beaten
2¼ to 2½ cups flour, sifted
Melted butter
Cinnamon and sugar mixture
Raisins
Chopped pecans

*Topping*
Melted butter
Brown sugar
Boiling water
Pecan halves

Dissolve yeast in sour cream. Cream the butter and sugar. Add the egg and the yeast mixture. Mix well. Gently blend in the flour. Refrigerate overnight, covered.

Divide dough in 2 parts. Roll out (half at a time) on a floured surface into a large rectangle. Brush with melted butter. Sprinkle liberally with cinnamon and sugar, raisins, and chopped pecans. Roll up carefully from wide end. Cut into 1-inch slices.

Place each slice into a muffin tin prepared with the topping. Let rise ¾ hour, covered, in warm place (70° to 80°).

Bake in a 350° oven for 20 to 25 minutes or until golden brown.

Makes 24 rolls.

*Topping:* Into each muffin pan cup, place 1 tablespoon melted butter, 1 tablespoon brown sugar, and a few drops boiling water. Mix together and add 2 or 3 pecan halves, bottom side up.

# June Wesbury's Danish Puff

BALABUSTAS: MORE FAVORITE RECIPES  B'NAI ISRAEL SISTERHOOD  GAINESVILLE, FLORIDA

1 cup butter or margarine
2 cups flour
2 tablespoons cold water
1 cup water
1 teaspoon almond
  flavoring, optional
3 eggs

Frosting
2 cups confectioners'
  sugar, sifted
1 tablespoon butter or
  margarine
4 tablespoons cream
1 teaspoon vanilla
⅛ teaspoon salt

Cut ½ cup butter into 1 cup flour. Add 2 tablespoons cold water. Divide dough in half and form each half into a 3 x 12 rectangle on an ungreased cookie sheet.

Place ½ cup butter in a pan. Add 1 cup water and bring to a boil. Add flavoring and remove from heat. Stir in 1 cup flour. Add eggs, one at a time, beating after each addition. Spread over rectangles.

Bake in a 400° oven for 50 minutes. Serve fresh and warm.

*Frosting:*  Beat sugar, butter, cream, vanilla, and salt. Frost danish while warm.

Serves 12 to 14.

# Yogurt Coffee Cake

THE MELTING POT  JEWISH COMMUNITY OF AMHERST  AMHERST, MASSACHUSETTS

½ cup butter
3 cups sugar
2 eggs, well beaten
2½ cups flour
1 teaspoon baking soda
⅛ teaspoon salt
1 cup plain yogurt
½ cup candied fruit,
  chopped
½ cup water
¼ cup orange juice
¼ cup ginger brandy or
  dark rum

In a large mixing bowl, cream butter and 2 cups sugar; add eggs and beat well.

Sift flour, baking soda, and salt and add to the creamed mixture alternately with yogurt. Fold in chopped fruit. Spoon into a well-greased 9-inch bundt pan.

Bake in a 350° oven for 1 hour.

Combine remaining 1 cup sugar with the water in a small pan. Heat slowly to dissolve sugar, then boil rapidly for 5 minutes. Add orange juice and brandy.

As soon as cake is done, remove from pan and place on rack over waxed paper. Spoon hot syrup over hot cake.

Serves 12 to 14.

* *This is a "never fail" cake! You may substitute 1 cup chopped nuts for candied fruit, if desired.*

# Apple Coffee Cake

COUNCIL'S COOK IN  NATIONAL COUNCIL OF JEWISH WOMEN  BAYSHORE, NEW JERSEY

6 apples, pared, cored, and sliced (about 3 cups)
5 tablespoons sugar
5 teaspoons cinnamon
3 cups flour
2 cups sugar
3 teaspoons baking powder
1 teaspoon salt
1 cup salad oil
4 eggs
¼ cup orange juice
1 tablespoon vanilla

Preheat oven to 375°.

Combine apples, 5 tablespoons sugar, and cinnamon and set aside.

Sift flour, 2 cups sugar, baking powder, and salt into a large bowl. Make a well in center and pour in oil, eggs, orange juice, and vanilla. Beat with wooden spoon until well blended.

Spoon ⅓ batter into a greased 9- or 10-inch angel food pan. Make a ring of ½ the apple mixture, drained of excess moisture, taking care to keep apples from touching sides of pan. Spoon another ⅓ batter over, make a ring of remaining apples, and top with remaining batter.

Bake for 1¼ hours or until done. Cover top with aluminum foil when it begins to overbrown.

Serve lukewarm with whipped cream.

Serves 12 to 14.

# Apple Nut Muffins

EDITORS' CHOICE

1½ cups firmly packed brown sugar
1 egg
⅔ cup vegetable oil
1 cup sour milk
1 teaspoon baking soda
½ teaspoon salt
1 teaspoon vanilla
2½ cups flour
1½ cups diced apples
½ cup chopped pecans
⅓ cup granulated sugar
2 teaspoons melted butter

Combine brown sugar, egg, and oil in a bowl. Combine milk, baking soda, salt and vanilla and add to brown sugar mixture alternately with flour. Mix well after each addition.

Fold in apples and nuts. Fill paper-lined or greased cupcake pans ½ full and sprinkle with the granulated sugar and butter, which have been mixed together.

Bake in 325° oven for 30 minutes or until tester comes out clean.

Makes 24 muffins.

* Delicious spread with cream cheese.

# Apple or Peach Cake

IN THE BEST OF TASTE   CONGREGATION BETH EL   SUDBURY, MASSACHUSETTS

1¾ cups flour
½ cup butter or margarine
2 teaspoons baking powder
1 teaspoon vanilla
1 egg
1 cup sugar
1 egg yolk
1 cup sour cream
¼ cup sugar
Confectioners' sugar (for peach pie)

*Apple Filling*
8 apples, peeled and sliced
½ to 1 cup sugar
2 tablespoons flour
1 teaspoon cinnamon
Lemon juice

*Peach Filling*
8 peaches, peeled and sliced
Lemon juice

Mix together the flour, butter, baking powder, vanilla, egg, and 1 cup sugar. Pat into a greased 9-inch pie plate. Cover with the prepared fruit.

Combine the egg yolk, sour cream, and ¼ cup sugar and pour the mixture over the fruit. (If you are using peaches, sprinkle confectioners' sugar over the top.)

Bake in a 350° oven for 45 minutes.

*To prepare the fruit:* For *apple cake*, combine sugar, flour, and cinnamon; mix with apples. Sprinkle with lemon juice. For *peach cake*, sprinkle lemon juice over sliced peaches.

Yield: 8 large portions.

* *This is delicious with whipped cream or ice cream.*


# Blueberry Muffins

THE CENTER TABLE   CONGREGATION MISHKAN TEFILA   NEWTON, MA

½ cup butter
1¼ cups sugar
2 eggs
2 cups flour
2 teaspoons baking powder
½ teaspoon salt
½ cup milk
2½ cups blueberries
Cinnamon-sugar (1½ tsp. cinnamon, 3 tsp. sugar)

Cream butter and sugar until fluffy. Add eggs, one at a time. Mix well after each addition. Sift flour, baking powder, and salt together; add to creamed mixture alternately with milk.

Mash ½ cup blueberries and stir in by hand. Add rest of blueberries whole and stir in by hand. Pour into greased and floured muffin tins (pile high). Sprinkle with cinnamon-sugar mixture.

Bake in a 375° oven for 25 to 30 minutes.

Makes 12 to 14 muffins.

* *This is the famous Jordan Marsh recipe.*

# Sour Milk Blueberry Muffins

SISTERHOOD COOKBOOK   BETH JACOB SYNAGOGUE   LEWISTON, MAINE

2 cups flour, sifted
2 teaspoons baking powder
½ teaspoon soda
½ teaspoon salt
2 tablespoons sugar
1 egg, beaten
1 cup sour milk
2 tablespoons melted butter
¾ cup blueberries

Sift flour, baking powder, soda, salt, and sugar. Add egg, milk, and melted butter. Mix thoroughly. Fold in blueberries. Pour into muffin tins.

Bake in a 400° oven for 25 minutes.

Makes 16 muffins.

* *To make 1 cup sour milk combine 1 cup milk with 1 tablespoon vinegar or lemon juice.*

# Blueberry Roll

CREATIVE COOKERY   TEMPLE SHAARE TEFILAH   NORWOOD, MASSACHUSETTS

1½ cups flour, sifted
2 teaspoons baking powder
½ teaspoon salt
2 tablespoons sugar
5 tablespoons shortening
1 egg
¼ cup milk (approximately)
1½ cups blueberries
¼ to ½ cup sugar (to taste)

Sift flour, baking powder, salt, and sugar into a large bowl. With pastry blender or 2 knives, cut in shortening until the mixture resembles coarse meal. Break egg into measuring cup and beat with fork; add milk to make ½ cup; blend well. Add to flour mixture, and stir quickly with fork until outside looks smooth.

Roll or pat out on a floured surface into an 8 x 10 rectangle. Cover dough evenly with blueberries, allowing 1-inch border along each side. (If using frozen blueberries, don't thaw.) Sprinkle sugar over blueberries. Starting at one long side, roll up like a jelly roll. Place in a greased 7 x 11 shallow pan.

Bake in a 400° oven for 20 to 25 minutes or until golden brown. Cut into slices.

Serves 12.

* *Delicious for breakfast or brunch. Not too sweet.*

# Maida Heatter's Peach Kuchen

FROM DORA WITH LOVE   SISTERHOOD OF GARDEN CITY JEWISH CENTER   GARDEN CITY, NEW YORK

*Dough*
1¼ cups all-purpose flour,
  sifted
¼ cup sugar
¼ teaspoon salt
¼ teaspoon baking powder
¼ cup butter
1 egg, slightly beaten

*Filling*
7 medium fresh peaches
  (about)
1 tablespoon flour
⅓ cup sugar
¾ teaspoon cinnamon
2 tablespoons butter

*Topping*
2 egg yolks, slightly beaten
¼ cup heavy cream

Sift flour, sugar, salt, and baking powder into a bowl. Using a pastry blender work in the butter until mixture looks like cornmeal. Stir in the egg with a fork. If the dough does not hold together, add 1 to 2 tablespoons of cream.

Transfer dough to a 9 x 9 pan. With floured hands pat the dough over the bottom and about 1¼ inches up the sides. See that it isn't too thick in the corners. This shell of dough may be frozen, or it may be filled and baked immediately.

Place the peaches in boiling water for a few seconds. Remove them to ice water. Peel and cut in quarters. Place in even rows over the dough, fitting them into each other very tightly, alternating direction (up one row and down the next). Mix the flour, sugar, and cinnamon and sift evenly over the peaches. Dot with the butter. Cover pan loosely with foil.

Bake in lower third of preheated 450° oven for 15 minutes.

For the topping, stir the yolks into the cream. Remove foil from kuchen. Without removing pan from oven, spoon the topping over the peaches. Reduce oven temperature to 375°. Bake 30 minutes longer, uncovered.

Cut into 9 or 10 portions. Serve warm or cold.

# Pineapple Coffee Cake

NUI WHAT'S COOKING  WOMEN'S LEAGUE OF YESHIVA  SPRING VALLEY, NEW YORK

2 cups flour, sifted
1 cup sugar, less 1
  tablespoon
2 teaspoons baking powder
⅛ teaspoon salt
½ cup butter or margarine
2 eggs
1 small can crushed
  pineapple, drained

In a large bowl, combine flour, sugar, baking powder, and salt; mix with butter until mealy. Reserve ½ cup for topping.

Beat eggs in another bowl. Add crushed pineapple and mix together. Add to batter and mix well, but not to a very fine consistency. Pour into an 8 x 10 or loaf-type pan. Spread with reserved topping.

Bake in a 350° oven for 35 to 40 minutes. Serve warm or cold.

Serves 8 to 10.

*If you prefer a more moist cake, use 3 eggs and 1 large can crushed pineapple, and bake in a 10-inch tube pan.*

# Pineapple Kugel

COOK ALONG WITH US  SISTERHOOD OF TEMPLE BETH SHALOM  PEABODY, MASSACHUSETTS

½ pint sour cream
4 ounces cream cheese,
  softened
3 eggs, slightly beaten
1 cup melted butter
2 teaspoons sugar
1 teaspoon salt
1 small can crushed
  pineapple, drained
½ pound wide noodles,
  cooked
2 cups cornflakes, crushed
Cinnamon and sugar
  mixture
¼ cup melted butter

Combine sour cream, cream cheese, eggs, butter, sugar, salt, and pineapple; mix with the noodles.

Pour in a greased 9 x 9 pan. Top with cornflake crumbs. Sprinkle with cinnamon and sugar. Pour melted butter over the top.

Bake in a 350° oven for 1 hour.

Serves 12.

* Rich and delicious!

# Prune Apricot Coffee Cake

ROCHESTER HADASSAH COOKBOOK   ROCHESTER HADASSAH   ROCHESTER, NEW YORK

¾ cup dried prunes
¾ cup dried apricots
2 cups flour, sifted
2 teaspoons baking powder
½ teaspoon salt
⅔ cup light brown sugar, packed
1 tablespoon flour
1 tablespoon cinnamon
¾ cup soft shortening
¾ cup granulated sugar
2 eggs
¾ cup milk
1 teaspoon vanilla
6 tablespoons melted butter or margarine
⅓ cup chopped walnuts

Soak prunes and apricots in hot water for 5 minutes. Drain fruit and chop fine. Set aside.

In medium bowl, sift 2 cups flour with baking powder and salt; set aside.

In small bowl, combine brown sugar, 1 tablespoon flour, and cinnamon. Mix well.

In large electric mixer bowl, at medium speed, beat shortening with granulated sugar until light and fluffy. Add eggs, one at a time, beating well after each addition. At low speed, beat in flour-baking powder-salt mixture alternately with milk and vanilla, beating just until combined. Gently fold in prunes and apricots.

Turn ⅓ batter into a lightly greased and floured 9-inch tube pan, spreading evenly. Sprinkle with ⅓ brown sugar mixture, then with 2 tablespoons melted butter. Repeat layering twice. Sprinkle chopped nuts over the top.

Bake in a preheated 350° oven for 55 minutes or until tester comes out clean. Cool in pan on wire rack about 25 minutes.

Serves 12 to 14.

# Fruit-Filled Coffee Cake
POT OF GOLD SISTERHOOD HAR SHALOM POTOMAC, MARYLAND

1 cup shortening
1½ cups sugar
3 eggs
3 cups flour
3 teaspoons baking powder
½ teaspoon baking soda
3 teaspoons vanilla
½ teaspoon almond extract
1 cup sour cream
2 teaspoons cinnamon,
  mixed with 2 tablespoons
  sugar
10 walnuts, chopped
1 can fruit pie filling

Cream shortening and sugar until light; add eggs, one at a time, beating after each addition.

Sift flour, baking powder, and baking soda. Add to creamed mixture. Mix well. Add vanilla, almond extract, and sour cream. Spoon half of the batter into a greased 10-inch tube pan.

Cover batter with ½ of the cinnamon-sugar mixture, then the chopped nuts and pie filling. Spoon in remaining batter. Sprinkle with the remaining cinnamon-sugar.

Bake in a preheated 350° oven for about 70 minutes or until top springs back when pressed. Let cool in pan before removing.

Serves 12 to 14.

*Variation: Spread half of the batter in a greased sheet pan (7½ x 11¾ or 9 x 13). Cover with a mixture of brown sugar, cinnamon, golden raisins, and chopped nuts. Cover with remaining batter, then sprinkle with cinnamon-sugar. Bake 50 to 60 minutes.*

# Orange Upside-Down French Toast
ALWAYS IN GOOD TASTE HAMPTON ROADS SECTION NCJW NEWPORT NEWS, VIRGINIA

¼ cup butter
⅓ cup sugar
¼ teaspoon cinnamon
1 teaspoon grated orange
  rind
4 eggs, slightly beaten
⅔ cup orange juice
8 slices firm white bread

Turn on oven to 400°. Place butter in a 10 x 15 pan and put into oven to melt. Remove from oven.

Combine sugar, cinnamon, and grated rind; sprinkle evenly in pan.

Mix eggs and juice. Dip bread in egg mixture, soaking well. Arrange evenly in pan; spoon any remaining liquid over bread.

Bake in a 400° oven about 25 minutes. Let stand 1 minute; then lift out and turn over (sugar side up) onto hot platter.

Makes 4 servings.

* *Toast can be frozen and reheated in oven. Good for children's breakfast.*

# Cheese Blintzes

EAT AND ENJOY   PHOENIX CHAPTER OF HADASSAH   PHOENIX, ARIZONA

*Filling*
**¾ pound farmers cheese**
**1 egg yolk, beaten**
**¼ teaspoon melted butter**
**½ teaspoon sugar**

*Batter*
**2 eggs**
**½ cup flour**
**½ teaspoon salt**
**½ cup milk**

Combine all filling ingredients. In another bowl, beat all batter ingredients together slowly until almost smooth. Refrigerate for at least 1 hour.

Lightly butter a hot 6- or 7- inch skillet. Tip the pan from side to side quickly so the batter spreads to cover bottom; pour excess back into mixing bowl. Cook on one side only for about 2 minutes or until batter loosens around sides of pan. Turn out, fried side up. Repeat until all batter is used.

Place rounded tablespoons of cheese mixture in center of each pancake (on the browned side), fold over from both sides, then into envelope shape.

Just before serving, fry on both sides until a golden brown. Serve hot with sour cream, applesauce, or sugar and cinnamon.

Makes about 12 blintzes.

# Muffin Blintzes

ESSEN 'N FRESSEN   SISTERHOOD OF CONGREGATION BETH CHAIM   EAST WINDSOR, NEW JERSEY

**12 ounces creamed cottage cheese**
**2 eggs, lightly beaten**
**½ cup flour**
**½ teaspoon baking powder**
**7 tablespoons sugar**
**2 tablespoons melted butter**
**Pinch salt**
**Dash *each* paprika, nutmeg**

Combine cottage cheese, eggs, flour, baking powder, sugar, butter, and salt; mix thoroughly. Fill (to the top) about 8 well-greased muffin cups. Top with dash each paprika and nutmeg.

Bake in a 350° oven about 1 hour. Muffins will puff up high while cooking but will drop back down. Can also be made day ahead and reheated.

Serve plain or with sour cream.

Makes 8.

* *Makes a good Shavuot or Yom Kippur break-fast.*

# Mini Blinis

KNISHES, GEFILTE FISHES AND OTHER JEWISH DISHES   TEMPLE ISRAEL SISTERHOOD   TALLAHASSEE, FLORIDA

16 ounces cream cheese
2 egg yolks
½ cup sugar
1 loaf thin-sliced white
  bread
1 cup melted butter
½ cup brown sugar
2 teaspoons cinnamon

Cream together cream cheese, egg yolks, and sugar. Cut crusts off bread and roll each slice with rolling pin until the consistency of dough.

Spread the cheese mixture on bread and roll up. Chill for a few minutes, then cut in thirds. Dip each piece in melted butter and then in mixture of brown sugar and cinnamon.

Bake in a 350° oven for 20 minutes.

Makes 48 to 60.

* *Serve as an appetizer or a dessert.*


# Blintz Souffle

FROM NIBBLES TO NOSHES   CONGREGATION AGUDATH ACHIM   SHREVEPORT, LOUISIANA

½ cup butter or margarine
12 frozen blintzes
2 cups sour cream
Pinch salt
6 eggs, beaten
2 tablespoons vanilla
3 tablespoons sugar
4 tablespoons orange juice

Melt butter in a 9 x 13 Pyrex baking pan. Roll each frozen blintz in the butter as you place it in the pan. Combine all remaining ingredients and pour over blintzes. Let stand at least 2 hours.

Bake in a 350° oven for 45 to 60 minutes.

Serves 12.


# Ice Cream Muffins

THE SPICE OF LIFE   B'NAI B'RITH WOMEN   UNION, NEW JERSEY

2 cups self-rising flour
2 cups vanilla ice cream,
  softened

Combine ingredients in a mixing bowl. Beat until smooth. Fill well-greased muffin cups ¾ full.

Bake in a 425° oven for 20 to 25 minutes.

Makes 12 cupcakes

* *If richer cake is desired, add 1 egg and 2 tablespoons cooking oil.*

# Mocha Sour Cream Cake
FAVORITE RECIPES   SISTERHOOD OF CONGREGATION BETH SHALOM   CLIFTON PARK, NEW YORK

1 cup butter, softened
1½ cups sugar
3 large or 4 medium eggs
3 cups flour
3 teaspoons baking powder
1 teaspoon salt
1 teaspoon baking soda
1 cup sour cream

*Filling*
1 package (12 oz.) chocolate
  chips
¾ cup brown sugar
3 tablespoons instant coffee
  (powder)

*Glaze*
2 tablespoons instant coffee
  (powder)
3 tablespoons boiling water
1¾ cups confectioners'
  sugar

Blend butter, sugar, and eggs together; add dry ingredients alternately with sour cream, and mix well. Combine filling ingredients in separate bowl.

Spoon ⅓ batter into greased and floured tube or bundt pan. Sprinkle with ½ of the filling. Cover with ⅓ more batter, then remaining filling, then last of batter.

Bake in a 350° oven for 1 hour 10 minutes. Cool. Cover with glaze.

*Glaze:* Dissolve coffee in boiling water. Add sugar and mix well. Spoon over cooled cake.

Serves 10 to 12.

# Chocolate Chip Coffee Ring
SUPER CHEF   BETH ISRAEL SISTERHOOD   WARREN, OHIO

1 cup sugar
¾ cup butter
2½ cups flour
1 cup sour cream
2 eggs
1 teaspoon baking powder
1 teaspoon baking soda
1 teaspoon vanilla
6-ounce package chocolate
  chips
½ cup light brown sugar
1½ teaspoons cocoa
½ cup chopped walnuts

Preheat oven to 350°. Grease a 9-inch tube pan.

In a large bowl, beat sugar with ½ cup butter. Add 2 cups flour, sour cream, eggs, baking powder, baking soda, and vanilla. After blended, beat for 3 minutes. Stir in ½ the chocolate chips; pour into pan.

In a medium bowl, combine ½ cup flour, brown sugar, and cocoa. With pastry blender, cut in ¼ cup butter. Stir in nuts and remaining chocolate chips. Crumble evenly over batter in pan.

Bake in a 350° oven for 60 to 65 minutes or until cake pulls away from sides of pan. Cool cake in pan on wire rack.

Serves 10 to 12.

# Chocolate Marble Yeast Cake

FROM DORA WITH LOVE  SISTERHOOD OF GARDEN CITY JEWISH CENTER   GARDEN CITY, NEW YORK

1 package dry yeast
½ cup warm milk
1 cup salted butter
½ cup sugar
1 egg
2 egg yolks
2½ cups flour

*Filling*
2 egg whites
½ cup sugar
2 tablespoons cocoa

Dissolve the yeast in warm milk; set aside.

Cream the butter and sugar. Add the egg and egg yolks and beat thoroughly. Add the flour alternately with the yeast mixture and blend thoroughly. Put into a bowl and place in refrigerator, uncovered, overnight.

The next day, prepare the filling. Beat the egg whites until stiff; add sugar gradually with the cocoa.

Roll out the dough to a rectangular shape about ½-inch thick on a floured pastry cloth. Spread with the filling and roll up as for a jelly roll. Put into a greased 9-inch tube pan or Bundt pan. Cover. Let rise in a warm place for about 2 hours until it is about double in bulk.

Bake in a 325° oven for about 1 hour or until done. Cool on a wire rack.

Serves 10 to 12.

# Cookies

## Glazed Fresh Apple Cookies

LIKE MAMA USED TO MAKE   ANN ARBOR CHAPTER OF HADASSAH   ANN ARBOR, MICHIGAN

2 cups flour, sifted
1 teaspoon soda
½ teaspoon salt
1 teaspoon cinnamon
1 teaspoon ground cloves,
   optional
½ teaspoon nutmeg
½ cup soft shortening
1⅓ cups brown sugar,
   packed
1 egg
¼ cup apple juice or milk
1 cup finely chopped apple
   (unpared)
1 cup chopped raisins
1 cup chopped nuts
Water

Sift flour, soda, salt, cinnamon, cloves, and nutmeg. In a large bowl, cream shortening and sugar; add egg. Add apple juice and then dry ingredients. Stir in fruits and nuts. Drop desired size on ungreased cookie sheet.

Bake in 350° oven for 12 to 15 minutes.

When cookies are cool, mix a little water with confectioners' sugar to make a glaze. Put a drop on each cookie.

Makes 40 to 50 cookies.

*Try baking this in a sheet. Cut into squares and dust with confectioners' sugar.*

# Lace Cookies

LEAVENED WITH LOVE   WASHINGTON HEBREW CONGREGATION   WASHINGTON, D.C.

½ cup butter, softened
1½ tablespoons flour
½ cup sugar
⅔ cup ground nuts
2 tablespoons milk
Pinch salt

In a small saucepan, combine all ingredients and stir over low heat. When well blended, measure 1 teaspoonful of dough for each cookie onto a Teflon or well-greased cookie sheet. They spread, so allow only 4 to 6 cookies on the cookie sheet.

Bake at 325° for 8 minutes. Remove from oven and "cook" (leave on pan) for 1 minute or less. Lift off with spatula onto waxed paper. Cool until crisp.

(Until you get used to lifting the cookies off the pan, I suggest baking only 2 or 3 at a time.)

# Oatmeal Lace Cookies

KITCHEN MAGIC   SISTERHOOD OF BET TORAH   MT. KISCO, NEW YORK

½ cup flour
½ cup sugar
½ teaspoon baking powder
½ cup oatmeal
2 tablespoons cream
2 tablespoons light corn
  syrup
⅓ cup melted butter or
  margarine
1 teaspoon vanilla

Sift together flour, sugar, and baking powder. Add oatmeal, cream, corn syrup, butter, and vanilla. Mix well and drop on very lightly greased baking sheets with a ¼ teaspoon.

Bake in a 375° oven for 6 to 8 minutes or until lightly browned. Let stand 30 seconds before removing. Drain on paper towel.

# Praline Cookies

THE FORT SHERIDAN AND GREAT LAKES JEWISH CHAPEL COOKBOOK   GREAT LAKES NTC   GREAT LAKES, ILLINOIS

1 egg
1 cup light brown sugar
1 cup chopped pecans
2 tablespoons flour
¼ cup melted butter

Beat egg. Blend in sugar. Stir in nuts and flour. Add butter and mix well. Cover a cookie sheet with greased foil. Drop small dabs from a spoon, widely spaced. They spread out tremendously.

Bake in a 350° oven about 10 minutes or until lightly browned. Let cool thoroughly before removing from sheet, or they will stick and be very gooey.

Makes 5 dozen.

# Sesame Praline Cookies

LEAVENED WITH LOVE   SISTERHOOD OF THE WASHINGTON HEBREW CONGREGATION   WASHINGTON, D.C.

¾ cup melted butter
1½ cups dark brown sugar,
  firmly packed
1 teaspoon vanilla
1 egg, beaten
½ cup sesame seeds
1 cup flour, sifted
¼ teaspoon salt

Combine butter, sugar, and vanilla. Beat until well blended. Stir in the egg and sesame seeds. Add the flour and salt and mix thoroughly. Drop by ½ teaspoonful onto a well-greased cookie sheet, 2 inches apart.

Bake in a preheated 350° oven for 4 to 5 minutes. Remove from cookie sheet quickly while cookies are warm. They will be thin and become crisp when cool. Store in a tightly covered container to keep crisp.

Makes about 100 small cookies.

# Pecan Puffs

ARTISTRY IN THE KITCHEN   TEMPLE WOMEN'S ASSOCIATION   CLEVELAND, OHIO

*Dough*
½ cup butter, room
  temperature
1 cup flour, sifted
1 cup ground pecans
3 tablespoons light brown
  sugar
1 teaspoon vanilla

*Frosting*
2 cups confectioners' sugar
1 tablespoon butter
2 tablespoons milk or
  cream
½ teaspoon vanilla
Food coloring, optional

*Dough:* Combine all ingredients and mix by hand. Taking a teaspoonful at a time, roll into balls. Make an indentation with finger. Place on lightly greased cookie sheet.

Bake in a 350° oven for 20 to 25 minutes.

*Frosting:* Combine sugar, butter, milk, and vanilla, and mix well. If desired, tint with vegetable coloring; divide frosting into sections and use a different color in each. Frost cookies after they are baked and cool.

Makes 25 puffs.

# Pecan Confections

CREATIVE COOKERY  TEMPLE SHAARE TEFILAH  NORWOOD, MASSACHUSETTS

1 egg white
1 cup brown sugar
1 tablespoon flour
⅛ teaspoon salt
1 cup chopped pecans

Beat the egg white to a stiff froth. Combine sugar, flour, and salt; add gradually to egg white. Fold in pecans. Drop by rounded teaspoon onto a greased cookie sheet.

Bake in a 300° oven for 15 minutes. Cool slightly before removing from cookie sheet.

Makes 2 dozen.


# Almond Macaroons

SISTERHOOD COOKERY  BROOKLYN HEIGHTS SYNAGOGUE  BROOKLYN, NEW YORK

4 egg yolks
1 cup sugar
2 cups ground almonds
Almond halves for garnish

Beat egg yolks. Add the sugar and beat again until lemon colored. Add ground almonds and mix well. Chill for several hours. Shape into small balls and arrange 1-inch apart on a well-greased cookie sheet. Top with almond halves.

Bake in a 350° oven for 10 to 12 minutes until golden.

Makes 48.

*This is the perfect answer to what to do with 4 egg yolks. (May also add 1 teaspoon almond extract, if desired.)*


# Tea Time Macaroons

FOOD FOR FUN  METROPOLITAN COUNCIL OF B'NAI B'RITH  NEW YORK, NEW YORK

2 egg whites
¼ teaspoon salt
¾ cup sugar
½ cup peanut butter

Beat egg whites with salt until foamy. Add sugar gradually, beating till stiff peaks form. Fold in peanut butter. Drop by rounded teaspoons 1 inch apart on a greased cookie sheet.

Bake in a 325° oven for 20 minutes or until lightly browned. Cool slightly before removing from pan.

Makes 2 dozen.

# Chocolate Macaroons

FROM GENERATION TO GENERATION  B'NAI AMOONA SISTERHOOD  ST. LOUIS, MISSOURI

12-ounce package
  semi-sweet chocolate
  chips
4 egg whites
1 teaspoon salt
1 teaspoon vanilla
½ cup sugar
3 cups coconut (½ lb.)

Melt chocolate over hot water. Beat the egg whites with salt until stiff; add vanilla. Add sugar gradually and beat until quite stiff. Add melted chocolate, then coconut. Drop from teaspoon onto a foil-covered cookie sheet.

Bake in a 325° oven for exactly 20 minutes.

Makes about 36.

# Meringue Kisses

SPICE OF LIFE  B'NAI B'RITH WOMEN  UNION, NEW JERSEY

4 egg whites, room
  temperature
1 cup sugar, sifted
½ teaspoon vanilla
6-ounce package chocolate
  chips

Heat oven to 250°. Cover ungreased cookie sheets with brown wrapping paper.

Beat egg whites until stiff enough to stand in peaks. Slowly beat in sugar, 1 tablespoon at a time. Fold in vanilla. Beat until stiff and glossy. Fold in chocolate chips.

Shape batter with a spoon into small mounds about 2 inches apart. Bake for 30 to 35 minutes. When cool, remove from pan with broad spatula.

Makes 50 to 60.

# Eir Kichel

THE COOKERY   TEMPLE BETH EL   SOUTH BEND, INDIANA

3 eggs
3 tablespoons sugar
½ cup oil
1 cup flour
Sugar

Beat eggs, sugar, and oil for 20 minutes at high speed on electric mixer. Add flour and continue beating for 5 to 10 minutes longer. Drop from teaspoon onto a greased cookie sheet about 2 inches apart. Sprinkle with sugar.

Bake in a 350° oven for 30 minutes or until brown. Light and delicious!

*Note: Very, very easy! Very economical! This recipe takes a beater with a strong motor. I believe that if it was done, for instance, in a heavy Kitchen-Aid using the kneading hook for the last 10 minutes it would be lighter and, for this recipe, the lighter the better. It is a non-sweet cookie for people who like something light. For a faster version, beat for 1 minute in food processor.*

# Kichel

EDITORS' CHOICE

3 large eggs
1 tablespoon water
1 tablespoon oil
2 teaspoons sugar
Pinch salt
4 cups flour (approx.)
Sugar for top

Beat the eggs until pale yellow, then add water, oil, sugar, and salt. Mix well. Add flour gradually to make a firm, dry ball. Pull apart and sprinkle with more flour, working in flour with the fingers. *Do not knead dough.*

Divide dough into 4 parts. Roll out each part until about ⅛-inch thick. Sprinkle lightly with sugar and roll it in lightly. Cut into diamonds 2½ x 1½ inches.

Preheat oven to 450°. Heat cookie sheet for 1 or 2 minutes, then place kichel on it and bake 5 to 10 minutes or until golden brown (watch carefully). Wash cookie sheet between batches. Cool and store in air-tight container.

Makes about 40.

*Exceptional treat, but set aside enough time for preparation.*

# Fluden
EDITORS' CHOICE

2 cups flour
¾ cup vegetable shortening
2 egg yolks
½ cup orange juice
½ teaspoon salt
½ teaspoon baking powder
6 tablespoons strawberry
  jam
2 tablespoons sugar
2 tablespoons cinnamon
1 cup chopped nuts

Mix flour, salt, and baking powder. Cut in shortening until crumbly. Mix orange juice and egg yolks together and add to flour mixture with a fork. Form into 2 balls, wrap, and chill for a few hours.

Place 1 ball on a floured board and roll out as thinly as possible into a rectangle. Spread ½ jam on bottom third of dough. Combine nuts, cinnamon, and sugar and sprinkle ½ mixture over entire rectangle and roll like a jelly roll. Repeat with second ball. Place on a lightly greased cookie sheet. Score top about every ½ inch.

Bake in a 350° oven for about 20 minutes. Slice while still warm.

Makes about 30 slices.

# Rosette's Rugalach
THE HAPPY COOKER   SISTERHOOD OF MALVERNE JEWISH CENTER   MALVERNE, NEW YORK

2 cups flour
1 cup unsalted butter
8 ounces cream cheese
⅓ cup sugar
1 tablespoon cinnamon
½ cup raisins
½ cup chopped walnuts

Combine flour, butter, and cream cheese. Mix well; form into 4 balls. Wrap each ball of dough in waxed paper. Refrigerate for at least 2 hours, preferably overnight.

Combine sugar, cinnamon, raisins, and walnuts for the filling. On a floured board, roll each ball into a circle ¼-inch thick and about 12 inches in diameter. Sprinkle with filling. Cut each round into 16 wedges; roll like crescents. Place on a greased baking sheet.

Bake in a 375° oven for 15 to 20 minutes.

Makes 64.

* For more petite rugalach, form dough into 8 balls and cut each ball into 12 wedges.

# Boulders

OUR FAVORITE RECIPES  HADASSAH AND TEMPLE JUDAH SISTERHOOD  CEDAR RAPIDS, IOWA

4 cups flour, sifted
2 tablespoons sugar
Pinch salt
2 cups butter
2 eggs, slightly beaten
¾ cup milk
1 package or 1 envelope
  yeast
Sugar-cinnamon mixture
Chopped nuts
Jelly
Raisins

Sift together flour, sugar, and salt. Cut in the butter. Add the eggs. Warm the milk and mix with the yeast until it is dissolved, then add to the flour mixture and beat well. Chill overnight.

Next morning, spread sugar-cinnamon mixture on a board. Form dough into round balls, about the size of a walnut. Flatten each into a circle and press into the sugar-cinnamon mixture. Keep turning into the mixture.

Put a little jelly, a few chopped nuts, and 3 or 4 raisins on each circle of dough. Fold into crescents. Place on ungreased cookie sheet, 10 to 12 at a time.

Bake in a 375° oven for 15 to 20 minutes.

Makes 80 to 90 cookies.

* Dough may also be rolled out and cut into 4-inch rounds.

# Butter Twists

COOK ALONG WITH US  SISTERHOOD OF BETH SHALOM  PEABODY, MASSACHUSETTS

1 cup butter
2 cups flour
1 egg yolk
¾ cup sour cream

*Topping*
¾ cup sugar
1 teaspoon cinnamon
1 cup chopped nuts

Cream butter; add the flour. Combine with egg yolk and sour cream. Chill 3 to 4 hours or overnight.

Divide dough into 3 parts. Roll each into a circle ⅛-inch thick. Cut each circle into 16 wedges.

Combine sugar, cinnamon, and nuts. Sprinkle on wedges and roll up each wedge toward the center.

Bake in a 375° oven 25 to 30 minutes.

Makes about 48 twists.

# Sour Cream Pastries

THE HAPPY COOKER  SISTERHOOD OF MALVERNE JEWISH CENTER  MALVERNE, NEW YORK

1 cup butter or margarine
2 cups all-purpose flour,
  sifted
1 egg yolk, beaten
1 cup dairy sour cream
½ cup apricot preserves
½ cup flaked coconut
¼ cup finely chopped
  pecans
Granulated sugar

With pastry blender, cut butter into flour till mixture resembles fine crumbs. Combine egg yolk and sour cream. Blend into flour mixture. Chill dough several hours or overnight.

Divide dough into 4 equal parts, keeping each part refrigerated until ready to use. Roll each part into a 10-inch circle on a lightly floured surface. Spread with 2 tablespoons of the apricot preserves; sprinkle with 2 tablespoons coconut and 1 tablespoon chopped nuts. Cut each circle into 12 wedges with fluted pastry wheel.

Starting from wide end, roll each wedge into a crescent. Sprinkle with a little sugar. Place on ungreased cookie sheet.

Bake in a 350° oven for 20 minutes or until lightly browned. Remove from sheet; cool on rack.

Makes 4 dozen.

* Very, very good!


# Lebkuchen

FAIRMOUNT TEMPLE COOKBOOK  FAIRMOUNT TEMPLE SISTERHOOD  CLEVELAND, OHIO

4 eggs
1 pound brown sugar
1 teaspoon vanilla
2 cups flour
2 teaspoons baking powder
1 scant teaspoon *each*
  allspice, cinnamon,
  nutmeg, ground cloves
1 cup chopped nuts
1 cup dates, cut up (or
  raisins)
Candied fruit, optional

Beat eggs and sugar; add vanilla, flour, baking powder, and spices. Blend well. Add nuts and dates. Candied fruit that has been floured may be added. Pour into a 10 x 15 pan.

Bake in a 325° oven for 30 minutes. Cut into strips while warm. Frost when cold with a thin glaze of confectioners' sugar, vanilla, and hot water.

Makes fifty 1-inch x 3-inch pieces.

# Tayglech

BALABUSTAS' — MORE FAVORITE RECIPES  B'NAI ISRAEL SISTERHOOD  GAINESVILLE, FLORIDA

4 eggs
3 tablespoons oil
2½ cups flour
1 teaspoon baking powder
1 pound honey
¾ cup sugar
½ pound pecans, quartered
1 tablespoon ground ginger
2 tablespoons water

Beat together eggs and oil. Sift flour and baking powder; add to the egg mixture and knead in the bowl until smooth. Pinch off pieces of dough and roll between the hands to form ropes ½ inch or less in diameter. Cut ropes into ½-inch pieces.

Bring honey and sugar to a rapid boil in a broad-bottomed ovenproof pan with a tight cover. Drop dough into boiling honey a few pieces at a time. Keep the honey boiling. When all pieces are in the pan, cover and boil 5 minutes. Remove from the flame; stir and cover.

Bake in a 375° oven for 30 to 45 minutes. Remove from oven and stir at 15 minute intervals. At the end of 30 minutes, test one of the tayglech by breaking it open with a fork. If it is crisp, it is done.

Add the nuts and ginger. Stir, cover, and return to the oven for 5 more minutes. Remove from the oven and sprinkle with the water.

Turn out onto a wet wooden board. Using a wet rolling pin or wooden spoon, gently spread tayglech to 1½-inch thickness. Dip hands in ice water and shape tayglech into a large square. Cool. Cut into squares or diamonds, using a sharp wet knife. Store in covered container.

Makes about 100 1½-inch square pieces.

# Hamantaschen

FROM DORA WITH LOVE  SISTERHOOD OF GARDEN CITY JEWISH CENTER  GARDEN CITY, NEW YORK

1½ cups shortening
1 cup sugar
2 eggs
½ cup orange juice
1 teaspoon vanilla
4 cups flour, sifted

*Filling*
1 cup poppy seeds
1 cup water
½ cup orange juice
½ cup pureed prunes
½ cup chopped walnuts
½ cup sugar
1 teaspoon grated lemon
  rind
1 teaspoon cinnamon
2 tablespoons bread crumbs
  or graham cracker crumbs
1 tablespoon margarine
  (parve)

Cream the shortening and sugar. Add eggs and keep creaming until smooth. Add orange juice and vanilla; stir in sifted flour and form into a ball. Place in a bowl; cover and chill overnight.

When ready to bake, roll out about ⅛-inch thick and cut into 3½-inch rounds, using a cup or a cookie cutter. Place a tablespoon of the filling in the center. Draw up two sides and then the third and pinch the edges together to form a three-cornered pocket. Place on a greased cookie sheet.

Bake in a 375° oven for about 30 minutes, until nicely browned.

Makes about 3 dozen.

*Filling:* In a covered saucepan, steam the poppy seeds in a cup of water for about 2 hours. Use a very low flame. Add a little more water if necessary. Drain. Grind, using the finest blade of the food chopper, or pound in a mortar until grayish in color. Mix with rest of the ingredients.


# Poppyseed Cookies (Moon Kichel)

FAIRMOUNT TEMPLE COOKBOOK  FAIRMOUNT TEMPLE SISTERHOOD  CLEVELAND, OHIO

8 tablespoons vegetable
  shortening
1 cup sugar
3 eggs, well beaten
3 cups flour
1 teaspoon baking powder
½ teaspoon salt
1 teaspoon vanilla
¼ cup ground poppyseed

Cream shortening and sugar together. Add eggs and blend thoroughly. Sift together flour, baking powder, and salt; add. Add vanilla and poppyseed and mix thoroughly. Roll to a ¼-inch thickness and cut with cookie cutter into desired shapes. Place on greased cookie sheet.

Bake in a 375° oven for 10 to 12 minutes or until lightly browned.

Makes 30 to 40.

# Culuria (Greek Cookies)

TRY IT, YOU'LL LIKE IT   TEMPLE BETH EL SISTERHOOD   RICHMOND, VIRGINIA

4 eggs
1 cup oil
1 cup sugar
2 teaspoons baking powder
Pinch baking soda
⅓ teaspoon cinnamon
2 teaspoons vanilla
6 cups flour (or more)
1 egg, beaten with some
  cinnamon
Sesame seeds

Combine eggs, oil, sugar, baking powder, baking soda, cinnamon, and vanilla, and mix until all the sugar is dissolved. Sift the flour into the mixture, and blend until dough is workable.

Pinch dough off into small pieces and roll between your fingers into a rope. Turn one end one way and the other end in the opposite direction to form an "s." Brush with egg and cinnamon mixture and sprinkle sesame seeds on top. Place on an ungreased cookie sheet.

Bake in a 325° oven for about 25 minutes or until brown.

Makes 40 to 50.

*These are authentic – and delicious!*

# Nut-Bread Cookies

EDITOR'S CHOICE

3 eggs
¾ cup sugar
¾ cup oil
1 teaspoon vanilla
1 teaspoon almond extract
3 cups flour, sifted
2 teaspoons baking powder
1 cup chopped walnuts

Beat eggs, sugar, and oil; add vanilla and almond extracts. Add flour and baking powder. Add nuts last.

The dough will be stiff.

With floured hands, shape dough into 3 or 4 loaves. (Three loaves will measure about 2 inches wide by 14 inches long.) Place on a greased cookie sheet.

Bake in a 350° oven for about 35 minutes. Cool enough to cut into 1-inch slices. Turn each slice on its side and brown in oven 15 minutes.

Makes 40 to 50 pieces.

*These may be sprinkled with a mixture of sugar and cinnamon, either before or after returning to oven for browning. Variation: Add 1 cup pitted dates cut in half and 1 cup maraschino cherries, cut in half. Mix with 2 tablespoons of flour and then mix into batter.*

# Mandel Brot

BALABUSTAS — MORE FAVORITE RECIPES   B'NAI ISRAEL CONGREGATION   GAINESVILLE, FLORIDA

1 cup sugar
¼ cup oil
2 eggs, well beaten
¼ teaspoon lemon extract
½ teaspoon vanilla
½ cup chopped almonds
2 cups flour, sifted
1½ teaspoons baking
  powder
½ teaspoon salt

Mix sugar and oil together; add eggs gradually. Add flavorings. Sift ½ cup flour over the chopped almonds and add to above; then add balance of dry ingredients. Pat with floured hands into 2 long loaves (2 inches wide by ¾ inches high). Place on a cookie sheet.

Bake in a 325° oven for 30 minutes. When cool, cut into slices ½-inch thick.

This cookie keeps well in a tightly covered can.

# Almond Slices

OUR FAVORITE RECIPES   TEMPLE JUDEAH   CEDAR RAPIDS, IOWA

3 eggs
¾ cup sugar
3 cups flour
1 rounded teaspoon baking
  powder
¾ cup vegetable oil or
  melted butter
1 teaspoon vanilla
1 teaspoon lemon extract
¾ to 1 cup chopped
  almonds
¾ cup white raisins
Cinnamon and sugar
  mixture

Cream together eggs and sugar. Add flour, baking powder, oil, vanilla, lemon extract, nuts, and raisins and mix thoroughly; dough will be very stiff. Shape into 3 long narrow rolls and place on cookie sheet.

Bake in a 350° oven for 20 to 30 minutes until lightly browned. Slice diagonally, place on cookie sheet cut side up; sprinkle with cinnamon and sugar. Return to oven and bake an additional 10 minutes.

Makes 5 dozen.

# Peanut Butter Cookies

COOK WITH TEMPLE BETH EMETH   TEMPLE BETH EMETH SISTERHOOD   ANN ARBOR, MICHIGAN

1 cup peanut butter
1 cup sugar
1 teaspoon vanilla
1 egg

Combine all ingredients. Roll into balls and place on an ungreased pan.

Bake in a 300° oven for 15 to 20 minutes.

Makes 2½ dozen cookies.

*This is an easy recipe for children to make.*

# Peanut Blossoms

COOKIE BOOK   TEMPLE ISRAEL SISTERHOOD   BINGHAMTON, NEW YORK

½ cup shortening
½ cup peanut butter
½ cup sugar
½ cup brown sugar,
  packed
1 egg
1 teaspoon vanilla
1¾ cups flour
1 teaspoon baking soda
½ teaspoon salt
Sugar for coating
Candy kisses (milk
  chocolate)

Cream shortening, peanut butter, and sugars. Add egg and vanilla. Beat well. Sift together flour, baking soda, and salt. Add to creamed mixture and blend thoroughly.

Shape the dough into balls and roll in sugar. Place on greased baking sheets.

Bake in a 375° oven for 10 minutes. Remove from the oven and top each cookie with a solid milk chocolate candy kiss, pressing down firmly so cookie cracks around the edge. Return to oven for 2 to 5 minutes until golden brown.

Makes about 36.

# Walnut Clusters

COOKIE BOOK   TEMPLE ISRAEL SISTERHOOD   BINGHAMTON, NEW YORK

¼ cup butter
½ cup sugar
1 egg
½ teaspoon vanilla
1½ squares baking
  chocolate, melted
½ cup flour
¼ teaspoon baking powder
½ teaspoon salt
2 cups broken walnuts

Preheat oven to 350°.

Cream butter and sugar. Add egg and vanilla, then melted chocolate.

Sift flour, baking powder, and salt; add to creamed mixture. Fold in walnuts.

Drop by teaspoon onto greased baking sheet. Bake for 10 minutes.

Makes about 48.

*These take a short time to prepare and are easy to handle.*

# Chocolate Chip Crescents

½ pound butter or
  margarine
¾ cup confectioners' sugar
3 teaspoons vanilla
2½ cups flour, sifted
6 ounces chocolate chips
7 ounces coconut
2 cups chopped pecans

Cream butter and sugar. Add vanilla and blend in flour. Work in rest of ingredients. Place about 1 tablespoon of mixture in palm of hand and roll into pencil shape. Shape into crescents and put on ungreased baking sheet.

Bake in a 350° oven for about 15 minutes until brown. Cool. Sprinkle with confectioners' sugar before serving.

Makes about 75.

* May be shaped into balls instead of crescents.

# Chocolate Chip Oatmeal Cookies
THE NEW PORTAL TO GOOD COOKING   WOMEN'S AMERICAN ORT, VIII   CHICAGO, ILLINOIS

½ cup soft shortening
6 tablespoons brown sugar
6 tablespoons granulated
  sugar
1 egg
¾ cup flour, sifted
½ teaspoon baking powder
½ teaspoon salt
½ cup chopped nuts
6-ounce package semi-sweet
  chocolate chips
1 cup quick-cooking rolled
  oats
½ teaspoon vanilla
Hot water

Cream shortening and sugars. Add egg and beat until very light and fluffy.

Sift together flour, baking powder, and salt. Blend into creamed mixture with nuts, chocolate, rolled oats, vanilla, and enough water to make a very stiff dough; blend just until mixed. Drop by rounded teaspoonfuls onto greased baking sheet, 2 inches apart.

Bake in a 375° oven for 12 minutes or until golden brown.

Makes about 3½ dozen cookies.

*1 cup of coconut may be added with nuts and chocolate.

# Chocolate Filled Snowballs

WORLD OF OUR FLAVORS   BETH HILLEL CONGREGATION   WILMETTE, ILLINOIS

1 cup butter
½ cup sugar
1 teaspoon vanilla
1 cup finely chopped nuts
2 cups all-purpose flour
1 large package Hershey's
  chocolate kisses
Confectioners' sugar

Beat butter, sugar, and vanilla until light and fluffy. Add nuts and flour; blend well and chill. Shape dough around the kisses, using about ½ tablespoon for each kiss. Roll dough into a ball and press kiss into it, covering completely. Place balls on an ungreased cookie sheet.

Bake in a 375° oven for 12 minutes, until set and slightly brown. Cool slightly and roll in confectioners' sugar while still warm. Cool.

Store in tightly covered container or freeze. Roll in sugar again, if desired.

Makes 5 to 6 dozen 1-inch balls. (Larger balls can be made, if desired.)

# Chocolate Crowned Acorn Cookies

THE HAPPY COOKER   SISTERHOOD OF MALVERNE JEWISH CENTER   MALVERNE, NEW YORK

1 cup butter
⅔ cup sugar
3 egg yolks
1 teaspoon almond extract
2½ cups flour
Green food coloring
Semi-sweet chocolate chips,
  melted (about 6 oz.)

Cream butter and sugar. Stir in egg yolks and almond extract. Add flour; stir until blended. Add 2 or 3 drops of green food coloring to make the dough a pretty green.

Pinch off small balls of dough. Roll between the palms of your hands into an acorn shape, pointed at the bottom. Place on a greased and floured cookie sheet about 2 inches apart.

Bake in a 375° oven for 10 minutes. Remove from oven and cool.

When cool, dip the wide end of each cookie into melted chocolate and place on waxed paper until chocolate has set.

Makes 50 to 60 cookies.

# French Truffles

COOKIE BOOK   TEMPLE ISRAEL SISTERHOOD   BINGHAMTON, NEW YORK

8-ounce package
  unsweetened baking
  chocolate
4-ounce package sweet
  cooking chocolate
1 can (14 oz.) sweetened
  condensed milk
Chopped pecans, chopped
  walnuts, or flaked
  coconut

Melt chocolates together over hot water. Add milk and mix until smooth and blended. Cool a few minutes, then shape into balls, using about 1 teaspoonful for each. Roll in nuts or coconut. Store in airtight container.

Makes 6 dozen.

# Chocolate-Covered Raisin Clusters

BALABUSTAS: MORE FAVORITE RECIPES   B'NAI ISRAEL SISTERHOOD   GAINESVILLE, FLORIDA

6-ounce package semi-sweet
  chocolate chips
3 tablespoons corn syrup
1 tablespoon water
1½ cups seedless raisins

In top of a double boiler, combine chocolate, corn syrup, and water. Heat over hot but not boiling water until chocolate is melted; stir until smooth. Remove from heat. Stir in raisins. Drop by teaspoons onto waxed paper. Chill until set.

Eat and don't go near the scales.

Makes about 36 small clusters.

*Drop into small paper candy cups.*

# Bourbon Balls

TRY IT — YOU'LL LIKE IT   JACKSONVILLE JEWISH CENTER SISTERHOOD   JACKSONVILLE, FLORIDA

2 tablespoons corn syrup
1 package vanilla wafers
  (7½ oz.), crushed
2 tablespoons cocoa
1½ cups confectioners'
  sugar
1 cup chopped pecans (or
  more)
3 ounces bourbon

Combine all ingredients. Form into balls (they will be sticky). Roll in confectioners' sugar and store in refrigerator.

Makes about 20 walnut-size balls.

*You may substitute rum for the bourbon.*

# No Bake Orange Balls
DELECTABLE COLLECTABLES  TEMPLE JUDEA SISTERHOOD  TARZANA, CALIFORNIA

1 box (7¼ oz.) vanilla
  wafers
¾ cup grated coconut
¾ cup (or less)
  confectioners' sugar
½ cup frozen orange juice
  concentrate, thawed

Crush wafers into fine crumbs. Mix crumbs, coconut, and sugar. Stir in orange juice. Form mixture into small balls and roll in additional confectioners' sugar. Store cookie balls in a tightly covered container overnight before serving.

Makes about 24 balls.

*More of a confection than a cookie.*

# Apricot Dainties
LEAVENED WITH LOVE  WASHINGTON HEBREW CONGREGATION SISTERHOOD  WASHINGTON, D.C.

½ cup butter or margarine
1 cup sugar
1 teaspoon lemon juice
2 eggs, separated
1 cup flour
½ teaspoon salt
¼ teaspoon baking powder
  or soda
1 jar (12 oz.) apricot
  preserves or jam
½ cup finely chopped
  pecans
Confectioners' sugar

Cream butter, ½ cup sugar, and lemon juice until fluffy. Add egg yolks, one at a time, beating well after each addition. Sift together flour, salt, and baking powder; add and blend well.

Spread batter into a greased 8 x 12 pan. Cover with a layer of the preserves.

Beat the egg whites until stiff but not dry; add ½ cup sugar gradually and continue beating until stiff peaks form. Fold in the nuts. Spread meringue over preserves.

Bake in a 350° oven for 45 minutes. Sprinkle with confectioners' sugar and cut into squares. Cool well before removing from pan. Can be frozen.

Makes about 2 dozen 2-inch squares.

# Pineapple Squares

FAIRMOUNT TEMPLE COOKBOOK  FAIRMOUNT TEMPLE  CLEVELAND, OHIO

1 cup butter
¾ cup sugar
2 cups flour
1 teaspoon baking powder
Pinch salt
1 egg, beaten
½ cup chopped walnuts
Rind of ½ lemon, grated
1 square unsweetened
  chocolate, grated
1 teaspoon vanilla

*Filling*
1 can (16 oz.) crushed
  pineapple, undrained
2 eggs
4 tablespoons flour
½ cup sugar
2 tablespoons lemon juice

Cream butter and sugar. Sift flour, baking powder, and salt, and add to creamed mixture. Add beaten egg, walnuts, lemon rind, chocolate, and vanilla. Pat into the bottom and up the sides of a 9 x 13 pan, making a shell. Do not bake.

Combine all filling ingredients in a saucepan and cook, stirring constantly, until thickened. Cool. Pour this custard into the shell. Sprinkle with additional grated chocolate.

Bake in a 350° oven for 45 minutes.

Makes about 24.

# Lemon Bars Deluxe

ALL THE RECIPES YOU WANTED TO BORROW BUT WERE AFRAID TO ASK  MIZRACHI WOMEN  OAK PARK, MICHIGAN

2¼ cups all-purpose flour,
  sifted
½ cup confectioners' sugar,
  sifted
1 cup butter or margarine
4 eggs, beaten
2 cups granulated sugar
⅓ cup lemon juice
½ teaspoon baking powder
Confectioners' sugar

Sift together 2 cups flour and the confectioners' sugar. Cut in butter until mixture clings together. Press into 9 x 13 pan.

Bake in a 350° oven for 20 to 25 minutes or until lightly browned.

Beat eggs, granulated sugar, and lemon juice. Sift together ¼ cup flour and the baking powder and stir into egg mixture. Pour over baked crust. Bake for 25 minutes longer.

Sprinkle with additional confectioners' sugar. Cool. Cut into bars.

Makes 30.

# Raspberry Bars

FAIRMOUNT TEMPLE COOKBOOK  FAIRMOUNT TEMPLE  CLEVELAND, OHIO

1 cup flour
1 teaspoon baking powder
Pinch salt
½ cup butter
2 tablespoons milk
1 egg
1 cup sugar
2 cups grated coconut
1 jar (8 oz.) raspberry jam

Sift flour, baking powder, and salt into a bowl. Cut in the butter and add milk. Knead very lightly. Press into a 10 x 10 pan.

Bake in a 350° oven 10 to 15 minutes until light brown.

While dough is baking, beat egg with sugar; fold in coconut.

Spread baked dough with jam, then with coconut mixture. Return to oven for 20 to 25 minutes until a very light brown. Cut into bars when cool.

Makes 25 two-inch squares.

# Hungarian Pastry Squares

ROCHESTER HADASSAH COOKBOOK  HADASSAH CHAPTER  ROCHESTER, NEW YORK

2 eggs, separated
½ cup butter or margarine
½ cup sugar
1 teaspoon vanilla
1½ cups flour, sifted
½ teaspoon baking powder
Pinch salt
Pinch baking soda
1 jar raspberry preserves
1 cup nuts, chopped

Beat egg whites until stiff but not dry. Set aside.

Cream butter and sugar. Add egg yolks; beat until light and fluffy. Add vanilla. Sift together flour, baking powder, salt, and soda; add.

Pat into a 9 x 13 pan. Spread with preserves, sprinkle with ½ the nuts, spread with beaten egg whites, sprinkle with the remaining nuts.

Bake in a 350° oven for 25 to 30 minutes. When cool, cut into squares.

Makes about 4 dozen 1½-inch squares.

# Peanut Butter Fingers

MENU MAGIC  BETH ISRAEL SISTERHOOD  FLINT, MICHIGAN

½ cup butter
½ cup sugar
½ cup brown sugar
1 egg
⅓ cup peanut butter
½ teaspoon baking soda
¼ teaspoon salt
½ teaspoon vanilla
1 cup flour
1 cup quick-cooking rolled
  oats
6-ounce package semi-sweet
  chocolate chips

Cream butter and sugars. Blend in egg, peanut butter, soda, salt, and vanilla. Stir in flour and rolled oats. Spread into a greased 9 x 13 pan.

Bake in a 350° oven for 15 to 20 minutes. Remove from oven and sprinkle *immediately* with chocolate chips. Let stand 5 minutes, then spread the chocolate. Cut into bars.

Makes 24 bars.

# Pecan Bars

BALABUSTAS—MORE FAVORITE RECIPES  B'NAI ISRAEL SISTERHOOD  GAINESVILLE, FLORIDA

½ cup butter
½ cup sugar
1 egg, well beaten
½ teaspoon vanilla
1¼ cups flour
⅛ teaspoon salt

*Pecan Layer*
2 eggs, beaten
1½ cups brown sugar
1½ cups chopped pecan
  meats
2 tablespoons corn syrup
2 tablespoons flour
1½ teaspoons baking
  powder
½ teaspoon salt
1 teaspoon vanilla

*Icing*
1½ cups confectioners'
  sugar
Lemon juice
Grated lemon rind,
  optional

Cream butter and sugar. Beat in egg. Add vanilla. Add flour and salt in three parts, blending well after each addition. Press dough into a 9 x 12 pan.

Bake in a 350° oven for 15 minutes.

Combine all the ingredients for the pecan layer. Spread over baked dough. Bake again for 25 minutes. Allow to cool.

For the icing, thin confectioners' sugar to spreading consistency with lemon juice. Add lemon rind, if desired. Spread over, and cut into bars.

Makes 24. Freezes well.

# Cheese Bars

WITH LOVE AND SPICE  SHOSHANA CHAPTER, AMERICAN MIZRACHI WOMEN  WEST HEMPSTEAD, NEW YORK

⅓ cup soft butter
⅓ cup brown sugar
1 cup flour (unsifted)
½ cup seedless raisins
½ cup chopped walnuts

*Topping*
8 ounces cream cheese
¼ cup sugar
1 egg
2 tablespoons milk
1 tablespoon lemon juice
½ teaspoon vanilla

Mix together butter, brown sugar, flour, raisins, and walnuts. Put aside 1 cup of mixture. Pack remainder on the bottom of a greased 8 x 8 pan.

Bake in a 350° oven for 15 minutes. Cool.

Mix topping ingredients. Spread over the baked dough. Crumble the remaining 1 cup of dough and sprinkle over the cheese layer.

Bake 30 minutes more. Cut into squares.

Makes 16.


# Cookie Crunch

THE NEW PORTAL TO GOOD COOKING  WOMEN'S AMERICAN ORT, VIII  CHICAGO, ILLINOIS

1 cup butter
1 cup sugar
1 egg, separated
2 cups flour, sifted
½ teaspoon cinnamon
¼ cup chopped nuts

Cream butter. Blend in sugar and egg yolk. Sift together flour and cinnamon; cut into butter mixture until mixture resembles coarse crumbs. Press into a 10½ x 15½ x 1 pan. Spread with unbeaten egg white; sprinkle with nuts.

Bake in a 350° oven for 30 minutes. Cut into squares while hot.

Makes about 3 dozen.


# Toffee Bars

PORTAL TO GOOD COOKING  WOMEN'S AMERICAN ORT, VIII  CHICAGO, ILLINOIS

½ cup butter, softened
¾ cup brown sugar, firmly packed
¼ cup sugar
1 egg yolk
½ cup quick-cooking rolled oats
½ cup flour, sifted
½ teaspoon vanilla
½ cup chopped nuts
½ cup semi-sweet chocolate chips

Cream butter and sugar. Add egg yolk and blend. Mix in rolled oats, flour, and vanilla. Fold in nuts. Press into a greased 9 x 9 pan.

Bake in a 350° oven for 15 to 20 minutes. Let stand a few minutes, then scatter chocolate chips over the top. Allow chocolate to melt; spread evenly with back of spoon. Cool. Cut into bars.

Makes 12 to 16 bars.

# Nanaimos

THE STUFFED BAGEL  HADASSAH CHAPTER  COLUMBIA, SOUTH CAROLINA

1 cup + 1 tablespoon
  butter
¼ cup granulated sugar
1 square unsweetened
  chocolate
1 teaspoon vanilla
1 egg, beaten
2 cups fine graham cracker
  crumbs
½ cup chopped pecans
1 cup flaked coconut
2 tablespoons instant
  vanilla pudding mix
3 tablespoons milk
2 cups confectioners' sugar
4 squares semi-sweet
  chocolate

Put ½ cup butter, granulated sugar, unsweetened chocolate, and vanilla in top of double boiler. Cook over boiling water until well blended. Add egg and cook 5 minutes longer, stirring. Add crumbs, nuts, and coconut. Press into a greased 9 x 9 pan. Cool. Chill 15 minutes.

Cream ½ cup butter until fluffy; beat in pudding mix and milk. Add confectioners' sugar gradually and beat until smooth. Spread over first layer. Chill 15 minutes.

Melt semi-sweet chocolate with 1 tablespoon butter. Spread over second layer. Chill until firm.

Cut into 1-inch squares. May keep in freezer until ready to serve.

Makes 81 squares.

# Sadie's Unusual Brownies

SUPER CHEF  BETH ISRAEL SISTERHOOD  WARREN, OHIO

1 cup butter or margarine
1 cup sugar: half brown,
  half white
2 eggs, separated
1 tablespoon water
1 tablespoon vanilla
2 cups flour
¼ teaspoon salt
1 teaspoon soda
6-ounce package chocolate
  chips
1 cup (about) chopped nuts
1 cup light brown sugar

Cream butter well; add sugar, a little at a time, and beat until light and fluffy. Add beaten egg yolks, water, and vanilla.

Sift together flour, salt, and soda, and add to creamed mixture. Spread in a greased 8 x 10 pan. Sprinkle with chocolate chips and nuts.

Beat egg whites until nearly stiff; slowly add light brown sugar. Beat until mixture stands up in peaks. Spread on top of other mixture.

Bake in a 350° oven for 30 to 35 minutes. Really easy!

Makes about 16.

*Some of the chocolate chips and nuts may be reserved to mix with the egg white mixture as a variation; also, a 9 x 12 pan may be used.*

*Testers' comments: "Quite unusual." "Great!"*

# Nutritious, Delicious Brownies

TRY IT — YOU'LL LIKE IT   JACKSONVILLE JEWISH CENTER   JACKSONVILLE, FLORIDA

½ cup vegetable shortening
1 cup sugar
1 teaspoon vanilla
2 eggs
1¼ cups all-purpose flour
¼ teaspoon baking soda
¾ cup chocolate syrup
½ cup raisins
½ cup wheat germ

Cream shortening and sugar until light and fluffy; add vanilla and mix. Add eggs, beating well after each addition.

Combine flour and baking soda; add alternately with chocolate syrup. Add raisins and wheat germ and mix all ingredients thoroughly. Pour into a greased 9 x 9 pan.

Bake in a 350° oven for 45 minutes or until done.

Makes about 25 brownies.

# Fudgie Scotch Squares

COOKIE BOOK   TEMPLE ISRAEL SISTERHOOD   BINGHAMTON, NEW YORK

1½ cups graham cracker
  crumbs
1 can sweetened condensed
  milk
6 ounces semi-sweet
  chocolate chips
6 ounces butterscotch chips
1 cup chopped nuts

Combine all ingredients and press into a very well-greased 9 x 9 pan.

Bake in a 350° oven for 30 to 35 minutes. Cool and cut into 1½-inch squares.

Makes 36.

# Honeybear Brownies

THE COOKERY   TEMPLE BETH EL   SOUTH BEND, INDIANA

⅓ cup butter or margarine
¾ cup sugar
½ cup honey
2 teaspoons vanilla
2 eggs
½ cup all-purpose flour
⅓ cup Hershey's cocoa
½ teaspoon salt
1 cup chopped nuts,
  optional

Cream butter and sugar in small mixer bowl; blend in honey and vanilla. Add eggs, one at a time, beating well after each addition.

Combine flour, cocoa, and salt; gradually add to creamed mixture. Stir in nuts. Pour into a greased 9 x 9 pan.

Bake in a 350° oven for 25 to 30 minutes. Cool and frost with your favorite frosting. Cut into squares. May be frozen.

Makes about 12 bars.

# Iced Chocolate Squares

LEAVENED WITH LOVE   WASHINGTON HEBREW CONGREGATION SISTERHOOD   WASHINGTON, D.C.

2 squares unsweetened
  chocolate
½ cup butter or margarine
2 eggs
1 cup sugar
½ cup flour, sifted
½ cup chopped pecans

*Icing*
4 tablespoons butter or
  margarine, softened
2 cups confectioners' sugar
2 tablespoons milk
½ teaspoon vanilla

*Glaze*
2 squares unsweetened
  chocolate
2 tablespoons butter

Melt chocolate and butter; cool slightly. Beat eggs until frothy, then stir in chocolate mixture. Add the sugar, then the flour and nuts. Turn into a greased 9 x 13 pan.

Bake in a 350° oven for 20 minutes. Allow to cool. Combine icing ingredients and spread on cookies. Chill for 10 minutes.

Prepare glaze by melting the chocolate with the butter. Spread cookies with glaze. Refrigerate for 20 minutes to harden glaze. Cut into squares.

Makes about 20 squares.

# Congo Squares

SECOND HELPINGS, PLEASE!   B'NAI B'RITH WOMEN   MONTREAL, QUEBEC

⅔ cup shortening
1 pound brown sugar
3 eggs
2¾ cups flour, sifted
2½ teaspoons baking
  powder
½ teaspoon salt
1 cup chopped walnuts
6-ounce package chocolate
  chips

*Chocolate Icing*
1 cup confectioners' sugar,
  sifted
1 tablespoon soft butter
2 tablespoons cocoa
2 tablespoons milk

Cream shortening and sugar. Beat in eggs. Stir in flour, baking powder, and salt, and blend thoroughly. Add nuts and chocolate chips. Spoon into a greased 9 x 13 baking pan.

Bake in a 350° oven for 45 minutes.

Cool. Ice with chocolate icing. Cut into bars.

*Chocolate Icing:* Combine all ingredients, and blend until smooth.

Makes 24 pieces.

# Coffee-Chocolate Brownies

COUNCIL'S COOK-IN  NATIONAL COUNCIL OF JEWISH WOMEN  BAYSHORE, NEW JERSEY

1 cup unsalted butter
2 cups sugar, sifted
4 eggs
1 cup all-purpose flour, sifted
4 squares unsweetened chocolate
½ cup strong black coffee
Chopped walnuts (about 1 cup)

Cream butter and sugar. Add eggs, one at a time, beating after each addition. Add flour and mix. Melt the chocolate in the coffee and add to mixture. Add nuts. Turn into a greased 8 x 10 baking dish.

Bake in a 350° oven about 25 minutes (test with toothpick). Cut in squares while hot.

Serves about 14.

# Fruit, ice cream, & other desserts

## Hot Fruit Casserole
SUPER CHEF   BETH ISRAEL TEMPLE CENTER   WARREN, OHIO

1 can pineapple chunks
1 can sliced pears
1 can sliced peaches
1 can plums, pitted
1 can dark cherries, pitted
1 can mandarin oranges
2 tablespoons brown sugar
½ cup blanched almonds
1 can (16 oz.) applesauce
1 teaspoon tapioca
½ cup sherry
12 vanilla wafers (about), crushed

Drain juices from fruits. Arrange in large casserole. Sprinkle with the brown sugar and almonds. Cover and refrigerate.

The next day, mix applesauce with tapioca and spread over fruit. Pour the sherry over all and top with the vanilla wafer crumbs.

Bake in a 350° oven for 45 minutes. Serve hot.

Serves 12 to 16.

* Use #2 cans when available. Quantities of each fruit can be varied according to personal preference.

# Fruit Tzimmis Flambe
KOSHER COOKING FOR EVERYONE   PLAINVIEW JEWISH CENTER   PLAINVIEW, NEW YORK

2 pounds dried fruit
 (raisins, pitted prunes,
 dried apricots)
1 cup orange juice
2 teaspoons sugar
1 cup water
½ cup rice (uncooked)
2 teaspoons Curacao
½ cup brandy

Wash fruit; drain. Combine orange juice, sugar, and water in a large pan and bring to a boil. Add fruit and rice and simmer for 20 minutes, covered. When rice is tender, stir in Curacao.

When ready to serve, sprinkle on the brandy and light.

Serves 10 to 12.

# Fruit Compote
EDITORS' CHOICE

1 bag dried prunes
1 bag dried apricots
1 can pineapple tidbits,
 drained
2 small cans mandarin
 oranges, drained
1 can cherry pie filling
½-1 teaspoon cinnamon, to
 taste
¾-1 cup pecans or walnuts
1 cup sherry

Place prunes on bottom of a well-greased 2-quart casserole. Then add the apricots, pineapple, oranges, and cherries. Sprinkle with cinnamon. Add the nuts evenly over the top, then pour sherry over the mixture.

Bake in a 350° oven until mixture bubbles. Serve warm or at room temperature.

Serves 10 to 12.

# Brandy Compote
BALABUSTAS — MORE FAVORITE RECIPES   B'NAI ISRAEL SISTERHOOD   GAINESVILLE, FLORIDA

2 large cans pear halves
1 large can peach halves
1 can apricots, pitted
1 large can black bing
 cherries, pitted
12 coconut macaroons
½ cup brown sugar
1 cup brandy, any flavor

Drain fruit thoroughly. Crumble macaroons and mix with sugar. In shallow dish, alternate layers of fruit with macaroon crumbs, reserving some crumbs for top. Pour brandy over the fruit and let stand 2 hours or more before baking.

Bake in a 350° oven for 1 hour. Serve hot.

Makes 12 to 18 servings.

# Tropical Compote
EDITORS' CHOICE

1 pineapple, cubed (about 4 cups)
3 bananas, sliced
2 packages frozen peaches (or fresh, if available)
1 cup dry white wine

Combine fruit with wine and marinate at room temperature for 1 hour. Chill for at least 1 hour.

Serves 8.

*Very refreshing after a large meal. Also makes a nice first course.*

# Strawberry Syllabub
EAT IN GOOD HEALTH   CONGREGATION B'NAI ISRAEL   ROCKVILLE, CONNECTICUT

1 cup strawberries, washed and hulled
3 tablespoons sugar
½ teaspoon grated orange rind
2 cups heavy cream
1 cup sliced strawberries

In electric blender, puree enough strawberries to make ⅔ cup. Mix puree, sugar, and orange rind in medium bowl.

Whip cream until stiff. Fold into strawberry mixture. Chill several hours.

Fold in sliced strawberries. Spoon into serving dishes.

Makes 8 servings.

# Apple Dessert

THE STUFFED BAGEL   HADASSAH CHAPTER   COLUMBIA, SOUTH CAROLINA

6 large apples
2 or 3 tablespoons sugar
¼ teaspoon cinnamon
1 cup flour
½ cup brown sugar, firmly
    packed
½ cup butter or margarine

Generously butter the sides and bottom of an 8 x 12 pan.

Peel apples, remove seeds, and cut into 8 wedges. Place the apple wedges in rows, as close together as possible, in a single layer in the pan. Mix sugar and cinnamon and sprinkle over apples.

Combine flour and brown sugar. Cut in butter and rub with fingers into crumbs. Sprinkle over and between apples and pat smooth.

Bake in a 425° oven for 30 minutes.

Serve hot or cold, plain, with ice cream, or with a small pitcher of milk to pour over servings.

Serves about 12.

*This is a Hungarian recipe, so good you should double the recipe and freeze half.*

# Pineapple-Lemon Angel Dessert

PALATE TREATS   MT. ZION TEMPLE SISTERHOOD   ST. PAUL, MINNESOTA

1 can (1 lb. 4 oz.) crushed
    pineapple
½ cup sugar
2 packages (3 oz. each)
    lemon gelatin
¾ cup orange juice
¼ cup lemon juice
1 pint heavy cream,
    whipped
10-inch angel food cake

Drain pineapple; reserve the juice. Add enough water to pineapple juice to make 3 cups; add sugar and bring to boil. Pour over gelatin in large bowl, stirring to dissolve. Add orange and lemon juices. Chill until thick, but not set.

Stir in pineapple. Fold in whipped cream.

Tear cake into 2-inch pieces. Pile ½ the cake pieces into a 10-inch tube pan. Spoon ½ the gelatin mixture over cake. Repeat the layers. Do not pack down.

Chill for 24 hours. Garnish with whipped cream, if desired.

Serves 12 to 14.

*Gooey and very good.*

# Heavenly Hash Dessert

BICENTENNIAL COOKBOOK  TEMPLE RODEF SHALOM  PORT ARTHUR, TEXAS

4 eggs
1½ (scant) cups sugar
4 heaping tablespoons flour
  (about ¾ cup)
1 pound dates, diced
2 teaspoons baking powder
2 teaspoons vanilla
2 cups chopped walnuts
2-3 large bananas
1 large can crushed
  pineapple with juice
Whipped cream
Walnuts, maraschino
  cherries for garnish

Beat the eggs until thick and lemon colored. Gradually beat in sugar. Combine flour and baking powder; add to dates and nuts. Mix. Add vanilla. Pour into 2 greased and floured 15½ x 10½ x 1 pans.

Bake in preheated 325° oven for 30 to 40 minutes.

When done, scrape out of pan onto foil. Let cool. (Do not worry if it breaks up.) Freeze one cake for later use.

Arrange broken pieces on round serving platter. Press pieces close together to form cake round. Cover with sliced bananas, then crushed pineapple over bananas. Top with whipped cream. Garnish with walnuts and maraschino cherries, cut into flowers. Refrigerate. (Put together in a.m. for p.m. dessert.)

Serves 20.

*"This is a gooey dessert, but delicious and refreshing. It has been my family's favorite for years. The base (torte) can be made ahead of time and kept in freezer."*

# Apple Latkes

THE SPICE AND SPIRIT OF KOSHER JEWISH COOKING  LUBAVITCH WOMEN'S ORGANIZATION, JUNIOR DIVISION
BROOKLYN, NEW YORK

4 apples
½ teaspoon cinnamon
3 tablespoons sugar
1 cup flour
1 teaspoon baking powder
¼ teaspoon salt
2 eggs, separated
3 tablespoons oil
6 ounces beer
Oil for frying
Confectioners' sugar

Peel and core apples. Cut into ¼-inch rings. Combine cinnamon and sugar and dip apple rings, coating well.

Sift flour, baking powder, and salt. Whip egg whites and set aside. Beat egg yolks; add with oil to flour mixture. Slowly pour in beer, mixing batter well until it becomes like snow. Then add the whipped egg whites and mix well.

Dip apple rings in batter and fry in small amount of hot oil. When done, sprinkle lightly with confectioners' sugar.

Serves 8 to 10.

# Peach Cobbler
BALABUSTAS — MORE FAVORITE RECIPES  B'NAI ISRAEL SISTERHOOD  GAINESVILLE, FLORIDA

2 cups sliced peaches,
  peeled
1¾ cups sugar
½ cup butter or margarine
¾ cup flour
2 teaspoons baking powder
Pinch salt
¾ cup milk

Set oven at 350°.

Combine peaches with ¾ cup sugar. Put butter in a large, very deep baking pan or dish (3 quarts) and place in oven to melt.

Make a batter of 1 cup sugar, flour, baking powder, salt, and milk. Pour over melted butter. *Do not stir.* Put the sugared peaches on top. *Do not stir.* Bake for 1 hour.

Batter will rise to top during baking and will be brown and crisp when cobbler is done. Serve with whipped cream or whipped topping, if desired.

Serves 6 to 8.

# Blueberry Buckle
THE CENTER TABLE COOKBOOK  CONGREGATION MISHKAN TEFILA  NEWTON, MASSACHUSETTS

½ cup shortening
1 cup sugar
1 egg, beaten
2½ cups flour
2½ teaspoons baking
  powder
¼ teaspoon salt
½ cup milk
1 teaspoon vanilla
2 cups fresh blueberries

*Topping*
½ cup sugar
½ cup flour
½ teaspoon cinnamon
¼ cup butter

Cream shortening and sugar. Add beaten egg and mix well. Sift flour, baking powder, and salt, and add to creamed mixture alternately with the milk and vanilla, which have been mixed together. Pour batter into a greased and floured 8 x 8 pan. Sprinkle the blueberries over top.

Combine ½ cup sugar, ½ cup flour, cinnamon, and butter, and mix until crumbly. Sprinkle over berries.

Bake in a 350° oven for 1 hour to 1 hour and 15 minutes.

May be served hot, warm, or cold.

Serves 12.

*\* Apples can be used in place of blueberries.*

# Sour Cream Strawberries

LIKE MAMA USED TO MAKE   ANN ARBOR CHAPTER OF HADASSAH   ANN ARBOR, MICHIGAN

1 pint fresh strawberries or
1 package (10 oz.) frozen
strawberries
½ cup sugar
1 pint sour cream
1 tablespoon lemon juice

Mix strawberries with sugar. Mix sour cream with lemon juice. Combine mixtures. Pour into freezer tray and freeze at least 3 hours before serving. Do not stir.

Serves 4.

# Cantaloupe Alaska

ABIGAIL SERVES   UNITED ORDER OF TRUE SISTERS   ALBANY, NEW YORK

2 cantaloupes, chilled
3 egg whites
Pinch salt
⅛ teaspoon cream of tartar
6 tablespoons sugar
1 pint vanilla ice cream

Halve cantaloupes and remove seeds. Scoop out fruit in balls. Return melon balls to shells and chill.

Beat egg whites and salt until foamy. Add cream of tartar and beat until stiff. Add sugar slowly, continuing to beat, until peaks are formed. Chill.

Heat oven very hot. Place filled cantaloupes in a pan of crushed ice or ice cubes. Top with a scoop of ice cream. Cover with meringue, which must cover top completely, and seal edges. Place in oven and bake 2 or 3 minutes until top is lightly browned. Serve immediately.

Serves 4.

* Variation: Halve cantaloupes; remove the seeds. Fill cavity with 1 to 2 teaspoons Crème de Mènthe, then a scoop of vanilla ice cream. Top with additional Crème de Mènthe, then meringue. Proceed as above.

# Baked Alaska
EDITOR'S CHOICE

2 grapefruit
4 teaspoons sugar (approx.)
2 egg whites
½ pint very hard vanilla
 ice cream
4 maraschino cherries

Cut grapefruit in half and remove dividers (membrane). Sprinkle with sugar (about 1 tablespoon). Beat egg whites with 1 teaspoon sugar until very stiff.

Place 1 scoop ice cream on each grapefruit half. Cover with meringue, making sure edges are sealed. Top with cherry.

Place in a baking dish. (A muffin tin will hold grapefruit upright.) Bake in hottest possible oven for 3 to 4 minutes to brown meringue. Serve at once.

Serves 4.

* *The perfect light dessert! Most people are surprised at how good grapefruit and ice cream taste together.*


# Cheri-Suisse Romanoff
GARDEN OF EATING   SISTERHOOD TEMPLE BETH OR   CLARK, NEW JERSEY

14 to 16 ounces pitted dark
 sweet cherries
1 cup heavy cream
¼ cup Cheri-Suisse (or
 other cherry liqueur)
1 pint vanilla ice cream,
 softened

Drain cherries. Whip cream with 2 tablespoons cherry liqueur. Fold into ice cream. Fold in cherries and 2 more tablespoons cherry liqueur.

Serves 8.


# Apricot Brandy Ice Cream
FAMILY FAVORITES   TEMPLE SOLEL SISTERHOOD   HOLLYWOOD, FLORIDA

1 package (10 oz.) frozen *or*
 1 pound fresh peaches
 plus 2 tablespoons sugar
1 pint peach ice cream,
 softened
3 ounces (6 tablespoons)
 apricot brandy

Whirl thawed peaches in blender or force through coarse sieve. (If fresh peaches are used, peel, slice, and add sugar; whirl in blender.) Combine peach puree with ice cream and stir in brandy. Work quickly, especially if fruit is not cold. Refreeze in bowl or parfait glasses.

Serves 4.

# Cantaloupe Ice Cream

ROCHESTER HADASSAH COOKBOOK   ROCHESTER HADASSAH   ROCHESTER, NEW YORK

½ cantaloupe
4 ounces evaporated
  skimmed milk, cold
Artificial sweetener to taste

Peel cantaloupe and cut into cubes. Place in freezer until frozen (about 24 hours). When frozen, put in blender with milk and sweetener. Blend until same consistency as soft ice cream. Can be stored in freezer.

Serves 4.

# Lemon Ice

SALT AND PEPPER TO TASTE   SISTERHOOD, CONGREGATION ANSHEI ISRAEL   TUCSON, ARIZONA

9 eggs, separated
1 cup sugar
1 large lemon, grated rind
  and juice

Beat egg whites with ½ cup sugar until stiff. Beat yolks with other ½ cup sugar; stir in lemon rind and juice. Fold yolk mixture into whites.

Pour into large (2-quart) bowl and put into freezer at once.

Serves 8 to 10.

*Good recipe for Passover.*

# Parve Ice Cream

FOOD FOR THOUGHT   TEMPLE SINAI   STAMFORD, CONNECTICUT

4 egg whites, room
  temperature
½ cup sugar
1 package (16 oz.) frozen
  berries, drained

Beat egg whites until stiff (approximately 20 minutes on high speed for hand mixer). Gradually add sugar; beat 10 minutes. Gradually add berries; beat 10 minutes.

Place 2 to 3 tablespoons of mixture into paper-lined muffin tins. Freeze.

Makes approximately 30.

*This really takes no time if you have a mixer that has its own stand rather than a hand mixer.*

# Ice Cream Cloaked in Chocolate

ONE MORE BITE  TEMPLE BETH ISRAEL SISTERHOOD  SAN DIEGO, CALIFORNIA

4 cups finely crushed
chocolate wafers
1 cup melted butter
2 tablespoons orange
liqueur
2 pints vanilla ice cream,
softened
2 pints pistachio ice cream,
softened
2 pints coffee ice cream,
softened
Coconut, fresh or flaked,
or chopped pistachio nuts

In medium bowl, combine crumbs, melted butter, and liqueur. Set aside ⅔ cup of mixture. Firmly press remaining crumb mixture over bottom and up sides of 9-inch springform pan. Freeze 30 minutes or until very firm.

Remove from freezer and quickly spread vanilla ice cream in an even layer over bottom. Sprinkle with ⅓ cup reserved crumbs. Freeze 30 minutes.

Repeat with pistachio and coffee ice creams. (Do not sprinkle crumbs on last layer.) Cover with foil and return to freezer.

To serve, invert pan onto chilled serving plate. Release latch and remove sides and bottom of pan. Garnish with coconut or pistachios. Cut in wedges with knife dipped in ice water.

Serves 12.

# Heath Bar Ice Cream Torte

THE SPORT OF COOKING  WOMEN'S AMERICAN ORT, VII  CLEVELAND, OHIO

½ gallon chocolate ice
cream
½ gallon coffee ice cream
1 ounce (or more) Crème
de Cacao
1 ounce (or more) Kahlua
3 boxes miniature Heath
bars, crushed (9–10 oz.
total)

*Sauce*
30 ounces prepared fudge
sauce
2 ounces Kahlua

Soften ice creams in refrigerator. Add Crème de Cacao to the chocolate ice cream and Kahlua to the coffee ice cream. Mix each thoroughly.

Lightly butter a springform pan. Line bottom and sides with crushed candy. Fill with alternating layers of chocolate ice cream, candy, and coffee ice cream, returning pan to the freezer after each layer so that layers do not mingle. Use thick layer of candy for the top. Return to freezer until firm, then unmold. Serve with Hot Fudge Sauce.

*Hot Fudge Sauce:* Combine fudge sauce with Kahlua and heat. (Quantities are approximate.)

Serves 12 or more.

# Grasshopper Ice Cream Pie

EAT IN GOOD HEALTH   CONGREGATION B'NAI ISRAEL   ROCKVILLE, CONNECTICUT

3 cups fine chocolate wafer crumbs
¾ cup butter or margarine, melted
2 tablespoons (2 envelopes) unflavored gelatin
¼ cup sugar
1½ cups water
½ cup green Crème de Mènthe
½ cup white Crème de Cacao
2 quarts vanilla ice cream, cut into chunks
1 cup heavy cream, whipped
Chocolate curls

Combine the chocolate crumbs and the butter. Divide in half and press firmly into two 9-inch pie plates. Chill until set, or bake at 325° for 10 minutes and then cool.

In a small saucepan, mix the gelatin with the sugar; add 1½ cups water. Heat and stir until gelatin is completely dissolved. Cool to lukewarm. Add the liqueurs and blend well. Chill again until thick and syrupy.

In a large mixing bowl, beat the ice cream until softened. Add the gelatin mixture and beat until well blended. Spoon into the crusts and freeze overnight.

Just before serving, top with whipped cream and garnish with chocolate curls.

Yield: 2 pies. Serves 16.

*This recipe can be successfully halved.*

# Fresh Strawberry Icebox Cake

ARTISTRY IN THE KITCHEN   TEMPLE WOMEN'S ASSOCIATION   CLEVELAND, OHIO

2 envelopes unflavored gelatin
½ cup cold water
1 cup mashed strawberries
1 cup sugar
2 cups whipping cream
1 tablespoon vanilla
1 cup sliced strawberries
2 dozen ladyfingers

Soften gelatin in cold water for 5 minutes. Dissolve over pan of hot water. Heat mashed berries with sugar until sugar is dissolved. Add gelatin and stir. Allow to cool.

Whip cream until stiff. Add vanilla. Fold gently into cooled gelatin mixture and blend well. Fold in sliced strawberries.

Line bottom and sides of a 10-inch springform pan with split ladyfingers. Add filling. Chill until firm.

Garnish with additional whipped cream and whole strawberries.

Serves about 10.

# Mandarin Icebox Delight

COOKS' CHOICE   BRANDEIS UNIVERSITY WOMEN'S COMMITTEE   WESTCHESTER SHORE, NEW YORK

3 eggs, separated
¼ cup granulated sugar
¼ cup milk
1 tablespoon cornstarch
½ cup unsalted butter
1¼ cups confectioners' sugar
1 orange, juice and grated rind
3 cups whipping cream
2 cans (11 oz. *each*) mandarin orange slices, drained
2½ dozen ladyfingers
1 teaspoon vanilla

Beat the egg yolks with granulated sugar until light and smooth. Put into double boiler with milk and cornstarch. Cook, stirring, until thickened. Turn into mixing bowl and cool.

Cream butter and 1 cup confectioners' sugar. Add orange juice and rind; blend. Add to custard and mix.

Beat egg whites until stiff. Beat 2 cups whipping cream until stiff. Fold egg whites into cream, then fold cream mixture into custard. Fold 1 can mandarin orange slices into mixture.

Line suitable dish or 9-inch springform pan with split ladyfingers. Pour in cream mixture. Top with whole ladyfingers. Chill several hours.

Serve with remaining whipped cream sweetened with ¼ cup confectioners' sugar and the vanilla. Top with remaining mandarin orange slices.

Serves 12 to 14.

# Rocky Road Cake I

WHAT'S COOKING AT SHIR AMI   CONGREGATION SHIR AMI   CASTRO VALLEY, CALIFORNIA

1 large angel food cake
12 ounces semi-sweet chocolate chips
1 or 2 tablespoons milk or cream
3 egg yolks
1 teaspoon vanilla
1 pint whipping cream
Chopped walnuts

Tear cake into bite-sized pieces and put into large pan (9 x 13) or 2 small square pans.

Melt chocolate chips in top of double boiler; add the milk. Add egg yolks and beat well. Remove from heat. Add vanilla.

Whip cream and fold into chocolate mixture. Pour over cake pieces in pan. Top with chopped walnuts. Chill 12 to 24 hours. (May be frozen.)

Serves 20.

# Rocky Road Cake II

FROM NOODLES TO STRUDELS  HADASSAH CHAPTER  BEVERLY HILLS, CALIFORNIA

12 ounces semi-sweet
  chocolate chips
¼ cup sugar
4 large eggs, separated
1 teaspoon vanilla
1 pint whipping cream
10-inch angel food cake,
  torn into bite-size pieces
1 cup chopped walnuts

Melt chocolate chips in a double boiler. Add sugar. Beat egg yolks and add slowly. Mix thoroughly. Add vanilla and remove from heat.

Beat whites until stiff but not dry. Fold into chocolate mixture. Beat cream until it forms soft peaks. Fold into chocolate mixture.

Grease a 10-inch springform pan. Cover bottom of pan with ⅓ the cake pieces. Add layers of ⅓ the chocolate mixture and ⅓ the nuts. Repeat twice, using up all of the ingredients. Keep in refrigerator overnight. Freeze. Let it set out 5 minutes before serving.

Serves 12.

* *This dessert tastes much better when served directly from freezer. It does not freeze solid and therefore is easy to serve.*

# Chocolate Mousse

EAT IN GOOD HEALTH  CONGREGATION B'NAI ISRAEL  ROCKVILLE, CONNECTICUT

12 ounces semi-sweet
  chocolate chips
10 tablespoons boiling
  water
8 eggs, separated
4 tablespoons rum or
  Grand Marnier
Ladyfingers, whipped
  cream (optional)

Mix chocolate and water in blender for 10 seconds. Add egg yolks and rum. Blend 10 seconds more. Pour into bowl.

Beat egg whites until very stiff and fold into chocolate mixture. Chill at least 1 hour.

Serve in a bowl lined with ladyfingers and topped with whipped cream.

Serves 10 to 12.

* *A "quickie" version may be made entirely in a food processor. Great for summer.*

# Instant Chocolate Mousse

ONE MORE BITE   TEMPLE BETH ISRAEL SISTERHOOD   SAN DIEGO, CALIFORNIA

¾ cup milk, hot
6-ounce package semi-sweet
  chocolate chips
2 eggs
2 tablespoons butter
1 tablespoon grated orange
  peel
3 to 4 tablespoons strong
  coffee (preferably
  Espresso) or 1 teaspoon
  finely ground powder
2 tablespoons orange-
  flavored liqueur (or more
  to taste)
1 tablespoon crème de
  menthe

Whip all ingredients together at high speed in blender until smooth and creamy. Pour into serving bowl or individual dishes. Chill 5 hours.

Serve plain or topped with whipped cream to which a little orange-flavored liqueur has been added.

Serves 6 to 8.

*This mousse is better than most 3-hour versions and takes only 5 minutes to prepare.*

# Chocolate Mousse — Pareve

BALABUSTAS — MORE FAVORITE RECIPES   B'NAI ISRAEL SISTERHOOD   GAINESVILLE, FLORIDA

½ pound dark sweet
  chocolate, cut into small
  pieces
6 tablespoons coffee or
  water
5 eggs, separated
2 tablespoons rum or
  Kahlua

Stir chocolate and coffee over low heat until chocolate melts. Do not let chocolate harden or burn. Remove from heat. Beat egg yolks until thick and lemon colored. Stir slowly into chocolate. Stir in the rum. Beat egg whites until stiff. Fold into chocolate mixture.

Pour into 8 small serving dishes or parfait glasses. Chill at least 4 hours.

Serves 8.

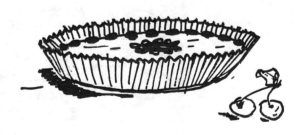

# Vandermint Mousse

GARDEN OF EATING  SISTERHOOD OF TEMPLE BETH OR  CLARK, NEW JERSEY

6-ounces semi-sweet
  chocolate chips
½ cup heated Vandermint
  (or any chocolate mint
  liqueur)
½ cup butter, softened
4 eggs, separated
2 tablespoons
  confectioners' sugar
Ladyfingers, optional

Heat the liqueur, then mix with chocolate chips in blender until chocolate melts. Add butter and egg yolks; blend again.

Beat egg whites and confectioners' sugar until stiff. Fold into chocolate mixture. Pour into dish lined with ladyfingers that have been dipped in—or brushed with—Vandermint. Or serve in individual ramekins or in a souffle dish without the ladyfingers. Flavor develops second day.

Serves 6.

# Rhubarb Mousse

BERKELEY JEWISH COOKBOOK  CONGREGATION BETH ISRAEL  BERKELEY, CALIFORNIA

1 tablespoon gelatin
  (unflavored)
¼ cup + 1 tablespoon
  white wine
2 cups rhubarb, cooked
  and sweetened
Dash salt
2 egg whites, beaten stiff

Lightly oil a 4-cup mold and rinse in cold water.

Soften gelatin in 1 tablespoon wine. Let stand 5 minutes, then dissolve in ¼ cup hot wine. Add cooled rhubarb and place in refrigerator until mixture just barely begins to gel.

Beat with wire whip or electric beater, add salt, fold in stiffly beaten egg whites, and transfer to mold. Refrigerate overnight. Unmold.

Serves 10 to 12.

# Lemon Souffle

FAVORITE RECIPES FROM OUR BEST COOKS   BETH SHALOM TEMPLE SISTERHOOD   DANVILLE, VIRGINIA

6 eggs, separated
2 cans (14 oz. each)
  sweetened condensed milk
5 lemons
Graham cracker crumbs
  (about ¼ cup)
Ladyfingers

Spread graham cracker crumbs on bottom of a 9-inch springform pan, then stand split ladyfingers around the side.

Beat egg yolks; add sweetened condensed milk. Beat again. Add juice and grated rind of lemons. Beat again. Fold in stiffly beaten egg whites. Pour mixture into pan.

Bake in a 400° oven for a few minutes until brown. Refrigerate overnight.

Serves 10.

# Lemon Cake Pudding

PLOTZ AND PANS   BETH ISRAEL SISTERHOOD   LANDSDALE, PENNSYLVANIA

¼ cup flour, sifted
1 cup sugar
¼ teaspoon salt
1½ teaspoons grated lemon
  rind
¼ cup lemon juice
2 eggs, separated
1 cup milk

Mix flour, sugar, and salt in a bowl. Stir in lemon rind, lemon juice, egg yolks, and milk. Beat egg whites until stiff; fold in. Pour into 1 quart casserole. Set in pan of water 1-inch deep.

Bake in a 350° oven for 50 minutes. Serve warm or cold. Top with whipped cream, if desired.

Serves 6.

* Orange juice and grated orange rind may be substituted for the lemon.

# Bread Pudding

THE WORK OF OUR HANDS   SISTERHOOD OF WESTCHESTER REFORM TEMPLE   WESTCHESTER, NEW YORK

4 cups white bread, not too
  fresh
2 eggs
Pinch salt
½ cup sugar
½ teaspoon cinnamon
2 cups milk
1 teaspoon vanilla
½ cup raisins
Nutmeg

Cut bread into cubes. Place in a greased 2-quart casserole. Beat eggs with salt, sugar, and cinnamon; add milk, vanilla, and raisins. Pour mixture over the bread and let stand for 10 minutes. Sprinkle with nutmeg.

Bake in a preheated 375° oven for 1 hour.

Serve warm or chilled, with cream.

Serves 8.

# Grape-Nuts Puff Pudding

WHAT'S COOKING  TEMPLE ISRAEL SISTERHOOD  CHARLOTTE, NORTH CAROLINA

4 tablespoons butter
1 teaspoon grated lemon
   rind
1 cup sugar
2 egg yolks, well beaten
3 tablespoons lemon juice
2 tablespoons flour
4 tablespoons Grape-Nuts
1 cup milk
2 egg whites, stiffly beaten

Combine butter and grated lemon rind and cream well; add sugar gradually, blending after each addition. Add egg yolks and beat thoroughly; stir in lemon juice. Add flour, Grape-Nuts, and milk, mixing well. Fold in egg whites. Turn into a greased 4-cup baking dish and place in pan of hot water.

Bake in a 325° oven for 1 hour and 15 minutes. When done, pudding has crust on top, jelly below.

Serve cold with cream.

Serves 6 to 8.


# Pumpkin Flan With Caramel Sauce

FAVORITE RECIPES  WOMEN OF BRIT SHALOM CONGREGATION  STATE COLLEGE, PENNSYLVANIA

4 eggs
½ cup sugar
½ teaspoon salt
½ teaspoon cinnamon
¼ teaspoon *each* ginger,
   allspice, nutmeg
1 cup light cream or milk
1 can canned pumpkin

*Caramel Sauce*
½ teaspoon brown sugar,
   firmly packed
1½ tablespoons water
1½ tablespoons butter
Pecan halves, optional
3 tablespoons dark rum,
   optional

Beat together eggs, sugar, salt, cinnamon, ginger, allspice, and nutmeg. Scald cream and beat immediately into egg mixture. Beat in pumpkin until smooth. Pour into a buttered 8-inch layer cake pan and place in a large flat pan with ½ inch hot water.

Bake in a 350° oven for 30 minutes or until firm. Cool to room temperature. Run knife around edge of pan and turn out into serving plate. Chill until serving time.

Combine brown sugar with water and butter. Bring to a boil and stir until the sugar is dissolved. Cool. Pour over the top of chilled flan and decorate with pecan halves. Serve in wedges.

To flame: Heat rum until it steams. Ignite and pour over flan.

Serves 6 to 8.

# Passover

## Passover Lemon Pie

ALL THIS AND KOSHER TOO   BETH DAVID SISTERHOOD   MIAMI, FLORIDA

4 egg yolks
1 teaspoon grated lemon
   peel
¼ cup lemon juice
¼ cup water
½ cup sugar
3 egg whites
6 tablespoons sugar

*Almond Matzo Crust*
½ cup ground almonds
½ cup matzo meal
2 tablespoons sugar
⅛ teaspoon salt
¼ cup peanut oil
1 egg white

In top of double boiler, beat egg yolks until thick. Gradually stir in lemon peel, lemon juice, water and ½ cup sugar. Cook over gently boiling water, stirring frequently until thickened, about 15 minutes. Remove from heat.

Beat egg whites until frothy. Gradually add remaining 6 tablespoons sugar, beating until soft peaks form. Fold ⅓ meringue into warm lemon mixture. Pour into cooled Almond Matzo Crust. Top with remaining meringue, sealing well to the crust.

Bake in a 325° oven for 25 to 30 minutes or until meringue is browned. Cool before serving.

*Crust:* Combine ground almonds, matzo meal, sugar, and salt. Combine peanut oil and egg white and beat slightly; stir into almond mixture. Press firmly and evenly against sides and bottom of a 9-inch pie plate.

Bake in a 325° oven for 10 to 12 minutes or until golden. Cool thoroughly.

Serves 6 to 8.

# Passover Apple Pie

FROM GENERATION TO GENERATION  B'NAI AMOONA SISTERHOOD  ST. LOUIS, MISSOURI

*Crust*
¾ cup matzo meal
¼ cup potato starch
½ cup sugar
⅓ cup oil
1 egg
Pinch cinnamon

*Filling*
3 or 4 apples, pared
Juice of ½ orange
Juice of ½ lemon
¾ cup sugar

Mix together all the ingredients for the crust. With hands, pat ½ the dough out into a thin crust on the bottom of a pie pan. Put the filling into the crust. Use remainder of dough by patting out little pieces for top crust.

Bake in a 350° oven for 1 hour.

*Filling:* Slice the apples thin and cook with the orange juice, lemon juice, and sugar for 10 minutes. Drain. Cinnamon may be added.

Serves 6 to 8.

# Wine Chocolate Nut Cake

MATZAH MAGIC  TEMPLE BETH EL SISTERHOOD  CHERRY HILL, NEW JERSEY

8 eggs, separated
1½ cups sugar
¾ cup matzah cake meal
2 tablespoons cocoa
½ cup finely chopped nuts
¼ cup sweet red wine

Beat egg whites with ½ cup sugar until stiff. Set aside.

Beat yolks with 1 cup sugar until thick. Add cake meal, cocoa, and nuts; mix well. Add wine and mix. Fold yolk mixture into whites, keeping them fluffy. Turn into an ungreased 10-inch tube pan.

Bake in a 325° oven for 50 minutes.

Serves 12 to 14.

# Passover Blueberry Cupcakes

ESSEN 'N FRESSEN  CONGREGATION BETH CHAIM SISTERHOOD  EAST WINDSOR, NEW JERSEY

½ cup shortening
1 cup sugar
½ cup matzo cake meal
¼ cup potato starch
¼ teaspoon salt
3 eggs
½ teaspoon orange juice
1 cup blueberries

Cream the shortening and sugar; set aside.

Sift together the cake meal, potato starch, and salt. Combine all ingredients and fold in blueberries. Place in large cupcake pans lined with cupcake papers.

Bake in a 350° oven for 50 minutes.

Makes 12 cupcakes.

# Apple Coffee Cake

MATZAH MAGIC   BETH EL SISTERHOOD   CHERRY HILL, NEW JERSEY

3 eggs, lightly beaten
¾ cup sugar
¾ cup matzah cake meal
⅓ cup peanut oil
Cinnamon-sugar mixture
5 apples, pared and sliced
⅓ cup raisins, optional

*Topping*
⅓ cup walnuts, chopped
½ cup sugar
2 teaspoons cinnamon

Lightly grease an 8 x 8 (or 9 x 9) pan.

Combine eggs, sugar, and cake meal. Add oil and mix well. Pour ½ mixture into pan. Sprinkle lightly with cinnamon and sugar mixture. Cover with ½ the apples and raisins. Repeat with remaining batter, apples, and raisins.

Combine the topping ingredients. Sprinkle on cake.

Bake in a 350° oven for 1 hour and 15 minutes. Cut into squares.

Makes 10 to 12 pieces.

*\* This is a Passover recipe that can be adapted to year-round use by substituting flour for the matzah cake meal. The recipe can be doubled, using a 9 x 13 baking pan.*

# Apple Squares

PASSOVER MADE EASY   EMANUEL SYNAGOGUE   WEST HARTFORD, CONNECTICUT

2 large apples
Cinnamon and sugar
  mixture
3 eggs, separated
1 cup sugar
1 lemon, juice and grated
  rind
½ cup oil
1 cup matzah meal
½ teaspoon salt

Peel and core apples, slice thin, and sprinkle with cinnamon-sugar mixture.

With electric mixer, beat egg yolks; add sugar gradually and beat until thick. Add lemon juice, lemon rind, and oil. With mixer at low speed, add matzah meal and salt.

Beat egg whites until stiff. Fold into egg yolk mixture. Pour half of batter into a greased 8 x 8 pan. Spread sliced apples on batter. Cover with remaining batter.

Bake in a 350° oven for 45 minutes or until nicely browned.

Serves 12.

# Passover Strudel

MENU MAGIC  BETH ISRAEL SISTERHOOD  FLINT, MICHIGAN

*Dough*
4 eggs
½ cup oil
2 cups matzo cake meal
1 cup potato starch
½ cup sugar
4 tablespoons cold water
Pinch salt

*Filling*
1 pound walnuts, chopped
2 large apples, grated
1 orange rind, grated
1 lemon rind, grated
2 tablespoons matzo meal
¾ cup sugar
1 tablespoon cinnamon
Jelly

*Glaze*
Beaten egg, optional

Beat eggs and stir in rest of the dough ingredients. Divide into 3 portions.

Mix together all ingredients for filling, except jelly.

Roll out one portion of dough, spread with jelly and ⅓ filling, and roll up. Repeat with rest of dough and filling.

Place on an oiled cookie sheet. Cut part-way through the rolled up strudels (at least ¾ down). Beaten egg may be brushed on top of the strudel before baking to give it a nice glaze.

Bake in a 350° oven for 1 hour. Slice through completely as soon as it is removed from oven.

Makes 36 pieces.


# Apricot Upside Down Charlotte

DO IT IN THE KITCHEN  WOMEN'S AMERICAN ORT, VI  HALLANDALE, FLORIDA

½ cup melted butter or
  margarine
⅓ cup brown sugar
8 apricot halves, drained
4 matzos, broken
1½ cups apricot nectar or
  juice
3 eggs
¼ cup sugar
¼ teaspoon salt
½ cup chopped nuts

In a 9-inch cake pan (springform preferred) combine 3 tablespoons of the melted butter with the brown sugar and spread evenly over the bottom. Place an apricot in the center, cut side down. Arrange remaining apricots in a circle ½ inch from the center.

Soak matzos in apricot juice at least 15 minutes. Add remaining butter, eggs, sugar, salt and nuts. Beat. Spread mixture over fruit in pan.

Bake in a 350° oven for 40 minutes. Loosen around edges and turn out immediately on plate. Chill.

Serves 8 to 10.

# Passover Mousse

THE SPORT OF COOKING   WOMEN'S AMERICAN ORT VII   CLEVELAND, OHIO

3 ounces semi-sweet
 chocolate (Passover
 chocolate bars may be
 used)
1 teaspoon coffee
4 eggs, separated
½ cup sugar
Sponge cake, day-old
Wine

Melt chocolate with coffee in double boiler. Beat egg yolks with ½ the sugar until fluffy; mix into the melted chocolate. Beat egg whites until foamy; gradually add the other ½ the sugar and beat until stiff. Gently fold into the chocolate mixture.

Cut sponge cake into small squares. Place the pieces in sherbet glasses and sprinkle with a little wine. Cover with chocolate mixture. Repeat until the glasses are filled and chocolate is the top layer. Refrigerate.

Serves 10 to 12.

*\* This same procedure can be done in a large glass bowl and served by the hostess. Top can be decorated if desired.*

# Banana Nut Farfel Pudding

WITH LOVE AND SPICE   SHOSHANA CHAPTER, MIZRACHI WOMEN   WEST HEMPSTEAD, NEW YORK

2 cups matzoh farfel
3 tablespoons oil
2 eggs
1 banana, sliced
⅓ cup sugar
¼ cup walnuts, chopped
½ teaspoon salt

Pour cold water over farfel in a colander. Drain at once, leaving farfel moist but not soggy.

Beat eggs. Blend into farfel. Add sugar, salt, and oil, stirring well. Add banana and nuts. Pour into a greased casserole.

Bake in a 350° oven for ½ hour, or until brown.

Serves 6.

*\* Variation: 1 large sliced apple may be substituted for the banana.*

# Passover Cookies

FROM GENERATION TO GENERATION   B'NAI AMOONA SISTERHOOD   ST. LOUIS, MISSOURI

2 egg whites
¾ cup sugar
2 tablespoons cocoa
¼ teaspoon salt
1 tablespoon orange juice
2 cups pecans, chopped

Beat egg whites until stiff but not dry. Combine sugar, cocoa, and salt; fold into egg whites. Transfer to a saucepan and stir over medium heat for 5 minutes. Cool at room temperature.

Blend in orange juice and nuts. Allowing ⅔ teaspoon for each cookie, drop onto foil-covered cookie sheet.

Bake in a 300° oven for about 30 minutes or until firm. Do not remove from foil until cookies are cold.

Makes about 4 dozen.

# Passover Fudge Squares

EDITOR'S CHOICE

4 eggs
2 cups sugar
1 cup oil
½ cup matzo cake meal
½ cup potato starch
½ teaspoon salt
4 tablespoons cocoa
2 cups pecans, chopped well

Put the eggs into a small mixer bowl and beat until mixed. Add the sugar and beat until the two are thick. With a spoon, mix in the oil.

Sift dry ingredients together, measuring without sifting first. Combine this with the first mixture and blend well; then fold in the nuts. Spread the batter into an oiled 9 x 9 pan.

Bake in a 325° oven for 35 minutes. Cool slightly and cut into 1½-inch squares.

Makes 32 pieces.

* These have a mild chocolate flavor and are rather crumbly.

# Passover Raisin Nut Cookies

EDITOR'S CHOICE

2 cups matzo meal
2 cups matzo farfel
1 teaspoon cinnamon
1½ cups sugar
4 eggs, well-beaten
⅔ cup oil
1 cup raisins
1 cup chopped nuts

Combine the matzo meal, farfel, cinnamon, and sugar. Add the eggs, oil, raisins, and nuts. Mix well and form into balls the size of large marbles. Put the batter balls on greased cookie sheets, not too far apart. They will not spread much.

Bake in a 350° oven for 15 to 20 minutes.

Makes 6 dozen.

* *Variation: add 1 cup coconut.*

# Chocolate Chip Cookies

MATZAH MAGIC   BETH EL SISTERHOOD   CHERRY HILL, NEW JERSEY

3 eggs
1 cup sugar
½ cup oil
3 tablespoons water
1 cup chopped semi-sweet chocolate
½ cup pecans, chopped
2 teaspoons grated orange peel
¼ teaspoon salt
2 cups matzah cake meal

Beat eggs and sugar until thick. Beat in oil with water till blended. Stir in chocolate, nuts, orange peel, and salt. Add the cake meal and stir until mixed. Let batter stand for 10 minutes to thicken.

Drop batter in 4 strips—about 12 inches long x 1½ inches wide—on baking sheets that have been oiled and lightly dusted with cake meal.

Bake in a 375° oven about 20 minutes until pale golden brown. Remove from oven; immediately cut each strip into diagonal slices, about ¾ inch wide. Remove from baking sheet and cool.

Makes about 5 dozen cookies.

# Passover Shortbread Cookies

FOOD FOR THOUGHT COOKBOOK   TEMPLE EMUNAH SISTERHOOD   LEXINGTON, MASSACHUSETTS

3 eggs
1¾ cups matzo meal
1 cup sugar
½ cup potato starch
1 cup peanut oil
Raspberry jam
Juice and rind of large
  lemon

Beat the eggs until frothy. Add the sugar slowly; continue beating. Slowly beat in oil, juice and rind; blend in matzo meal and starch, beating all the while. Drop by teaspoonful onto greased cookie sheet and place ½ teaspoon raspberry jam in the center of each cookie.

Bake in a 350° oven for 20 to 25 minutes. Remove from pan immediately and cool on a rack.

Makes about 4 dozen.

# Passover Blintzes

FOOD FOR THOUGHT   TEMPLE EMUNAH SISTERHOOD   LEXINGTON, MASSACHUSETTS

2 tablespoons plus 1
  teaspoon potato starch
½ teaspoon salt
1 cup water
2 eggs, beaten
Fat for frying

*Filling*
2 onions, minced
3 tablespoons chicken fat
1 pound chicken livers or
  calves liver
2 eggs, lightly beaten
2 tablespoons matzo meal
Salt and pepper to taste

Dissolve the potato starch and salt in water. Add the eggs and mix thoroughly.

Heat a 10-inch skillet. Coat lightly with fat. Pour a small amount of batter into hot skillet, tipping the skillet around so that it is evenly coated with the mixture. Pour any excess back into mixing bowl. Brown lightly on each side.

Spoon filling into blintzes. Fold up sides and roll up so all filling is sealed in. Place in a greased baking dish.

Bake in a 325° oven for 20 to 25 minutes.

*Filling:* Sauté onions in fat until transparent; set aside. Broil liver; do not allow to become too dry. Grind liver and add to onions. Combine remaining ingredients and add to the liver; blend thoroughly.

Makes 8 large blintzes.

*Any left over meat or chicken can be ground and used in place of liver. Do not double recipe as potato starch settles and will not thicken properly.*

# Passover Candy

SISTERHOOD COOKERY   BROOKLYN HEIGHTS SYNAGOGUE SISTERHOOD   BROOKLYN, NEW YORK

4 cups matzoh farfel
4 eggs, slightly beaten
1½ pounds honey
¾ cup sugar
1 pound walnuts, broken
  into pieces
Ground ginger

Combine farfel and eggs and refrigerate overnight.

Bring honey and sugar to a boil; break the farfel mixture into small pieces as you slowly add it to the boiling honey. Stir constantly with a wooden spoon until the farfel begins to toast. Add walnuts. Continue stirring until all the honey is absorbed. It should be the color of Taiglach (honey-colored).

Turn out on a wet board. When cool enough to handle, wet hands and flatten out until it is about 1-inch thick. Sprinkle with ginger. Cut into 1-inch squares when cold.

Serves 18 to 20.

# Hints

## Quick and easy

There are times when you have only a few minutes to prepare something delicious to serve to your guests. Here are some suggestions that are easy to prepare. Other time-saving recipes are listed in the index under "Ten Minute Recipes."

| | |
|---|---|
| Anchovy filets, canned | (1) Serve on crackers.<br>(2) Mash into softened cheese with a little lemon juice; pile on toast and place under broiler until the cheese bubbles. |
| Anchovy paste | Blend 4 tablespoons anchovy paste with 2 tablespoons horseradish, 1½ tablespoons lemon juice and ¾ cup whipped cream. Heap on rounds of toast. |
| Caviar | (1) Serve on toast or crackers with finely chopped hard-boiled eggs and onions.<br>(2) Mix 2 tablespoons caviar with 4 tablespoons cream cheese and 1 teaspoon finely chopped green onion; serve with crackers. |
| Celery | (1) Stuff with mixture of cream cheese, a little mayonnaise, minced ripe or stuffed olives, seasoned to taste with minced onion, salt, and pepper.<br>(2) Stuff with cream cheese and Roquefort cheese, moistened with a little cream and seasoned to taste.<br>(3) Stuff with a mixture of ½ cup grated cheddar cheese, 2 tablespoons sour cream, 1 tablespoon horseradish, 2 tablespoons coarsely grated nuts, 1 tablespoon lemon juice, and salt and pepper to taste. |

(4) Stuff with a mixture of Roquefort or bleu cheese, chopped stuffed olives, a little Worcestershire sauce, and mayonnaise.

(5) Stuff with mashed avocado seasoned with lemon juice, salt, and a dash of grated onion.

**Cheese**

(1) Combine 1 cup grated cheese, ½ teaspoon onion juice, and a pinch of tarragon; moisten with mayonnaise and serve with crackers.

(2) Blend grated Italian style cheese with mayonnaise to make a very thick mixture; place a paper-thin slice of onion on a round of bread, heap with mixture, dust with paprika and place under broiler until the bread is toasted and the top bubbles.

(3) Mash together until smooth 3 ounces cream cheese, ½ cup crumbled Roquefort or bleu cheese, ½ cup mayonnaise, and 1 tablespoon Worcestershire sauce; serve with crackers.

**Chutney**

(1) Serve a bowl of chutney on a small tray surrounded by assorted cheeses and crackers.

(2) Dice chutney very fine and spread on bread rounds that have been fried on the opposite side. Cover with a thin slice of cheddar cheese, then pop under broiler until cheese is melted. Cut each circle in half and decorate with a pickled onion.

**Cottage cheese**

Combine 1 pint cottage cheese with 2 tablespoons finely minced parsley, 2 finely chopped green onions (tops and all), 1 tablespoon horseradish, 2 tablespoons mayonnaise, 1 tablespoon Worcestershire sauce, dash Tabasco, and salt and pepper to taste. Serve with crackers or as a potato chip dip.

**Cream cheese**

(1) Smoked fish and many kinds of vegetables (raw or cooked), can be chopped and mixed with cream cheese seasoned to taste with Worcestershire, Tabasco, seasoned salt, sauces, etc., for some delicious combinations. (Experiment with leftovers.) Let rest for several hours to allow flavors to mix. Serve with crackers.

(2) Cover a block of cream cheese with caviar, or Worcestershire, or chutney. Serve with crackers.

(3) Mix Worcestershire sauce with softened cheese and fill raw mushroom caps.

| | |
|---|---|
| Fruit, canned or frozen | Mix assorted fruits with any of the following: fresh fruit, shredded coconut, fruit liqueur, or cinnamon; serve alone or as topping for ice cream, cake, or pudding. |
| Fruit juices | Add Tabasco, Worcestershire, and celery salt to tomato juice for a first course; combine orange and pineapple or pineapple and grapefruit for a new taste. |
| Ice cream | (1) Can be topped with fruit or liqueur or both.<br>(2) Add ⅓ cup liqueur to 1 quart softened ice cream, mix and refreeze; or mix in blender for a "frostee."<br>(3) Soften and spoon into a pie crust; refreeze and top with fruit sauce and whipped topping; sprinkle with chopped nuts. |
| Meat, leftovers | Chop pieces of cold chicken or beef with food chopper or food processor; add:<br>(1) chopped chives, mayonnaise and a few diced nut meats to taste;<br>(2) add prepared Worcestershire sauce and some diced green olives to taste; heap on rounds or strips of toasted bread or serve with crackers. |
| Mushroom caps, fresh or canned | (1) Fill with leftovers (chopped), mixed with bread or cracker crumbs; top with more crumbs and brown under broiler. In some cases you may want to top with Parmesan cheese before browning.<br>(2) Fill with small pieces of sharp cheese and dot with butter or margarine; broil slowly until cheese is melted and mushrooms are cooked through. Spear each mushroom on a toothpick and serve immediately. |
| Olives, chopped | (1) Blend with enough mayonnaise to give a spreadable consistency. Season to taste with salt, pepper, and minced onion, and serve with crackers or potato chips.<br>(2) Blend with chopped hard-boiled egg and mayonnaise to taste. Serve as a canape on fresh bread or toast rounds. |
| Onion soup, dried | Mix with yogurt, sour cream, or cottage cheese for a dip. |

| | |
|---|---|
| Puddings, packaged | (1) Top with fruit (fresh, canned, or frozen) or liqueur.<br>(2) Fill a ready-made pie crust and serve with whipped topping and/or fruit or canned fruit pie filling.<br>(3) Make a mocha pudding by substituting 1 cup cream and 1 cup strong coffee for the usual 2 cups milk in chocolate pudding. |
| Salmon or tuna, canned | Combine with mayonnaise and spices to taste. Spread on crackers. |
| Sardines, canned | (1) Place over an onion ring on buttered party rye.<br>(2) Drain on paper towel. Cover with English mustard, sprinkle with bread crumbs, and season with a few drops of lemon juice. Broil for a few minutes, then place on fingers of lightly buttered rye toast. Serve hot. |
| Sour cream | (1) Good for dip mixtures — see "cottage cheese" and "cream cheese" above.<br>(2) Use as a dessert topping or combine with fruit. |
| Vegetables, fresh | Carrots, celery, cucumbers, radishes, green onions, radishes, bell peppers, asparagus, cauliflower, etc. all make good nibbles and "dippers." |
| Yogurt, plain | (1) Good for dip mixtures (mix with pickle relish or chopped olives); see "cottage cheese" and "cream cheese" above.<br>(2) Use as dessert topping or combine with fruit. |

# Emergency substitutions

Baking powder | 1 teaspoon = ¼ teaspoon baking soda plus ½ teaspoon cream of tartar

Catsup | 1 cup = 1 cup tomato sauce and 2 tablespoons sugar plus 1 tablespoons vinegar

Chocolate | 1-ounce square = 3 tablespoons cocoa plus ½ tablespoon butter

Cornstarch | 1 tablespoon = 2 tablespoons flour *or* 4 teaspoons quick cooking tapioca

Cream | 1 cup = 1 cup undiluted evaporated milk *or* 14 tablespoons milk plus 2 tablespoons butter or margarine

Egg | 1 whole egg = 2 egg yolks

Flour, all-purpose *(for thickening)* | 1 tablespoon = ½ teaspoon cornstarch, potato starch, rice starch, or arrowroot starch, *or* 1 tablespoon tapioca.

Flour, cake | 1 cup = 1 cup less 2 tablespoons all-purpose flour

Garlic | 1 clove = ⅛ teaspoon minced dried garlic or garlic powder

Herbs | 1 tablespoon fresh chopped = 1 teaspoon dried crushed *or* ½ teaspoon ground herbs

Milk | 1 cup = ½ cup evaporated milk plus ½ cup water

Onion | 1 medium = 1 tablespoon minced dried onion *or* 1 teaspoon onion powder

Sour cream | 8 ounces = 8 ounces yogurt *or* 6 ounces cream cheese plus 3 tablespoons milk

Sour milk | 1 cup = 1 cup milk plus 1 tablespoon vinegar or lemon juice

Stuffing | 8-ounce package = 4 cups croutons

Sugar | 1 cup = 1 cup packed brown sugar *or* 2 cups sifted powdered sugar. *Do not substitute powdered sugar in baking.*

Tomatoes | 3 fresh medium = 16-ounce can whole or stewed

Tomato sauce | 15-ounce can = 6-ounce can tomato paste plus 1 cup water

# A prepared pantry

*Staples:* baking powder, baking soda, chocolate (unsweetened), cocoa, cornstarch, evaporated milk, flour, gelatin (unflavored), seasonings (allspice, basil, bay leaf, cayenne, chile powder, cinnamon, cloves, curry powder, garlic/garlic powder, ginger, mustard, nutmeg, paprika, thyme), oil (salad, olive), pepper, salt, shortening, sugar (brown, confectioners', granulated), vanilla.

*Pantry:* anchovy paste, artichoke hearts, Boston brown bread, capers, catsup, caviar, chick peas, chocolate chips, chutney, coconut, coffee, cookies, corn chips, crackers, date-nut bread, dried fruit, canned fish (tuna, salmon, sardines), canned fruit, gelatin (flavored), fruit juice, honey, jelly, mushrooms (canned), mustard (prepared), nuts, olives (stuffed, ripe, chopped), onion soup mix, peanut butter, pickles, fruit pie fillings (canned), nuts, popcorn, potato chips, pretzels, pudding mix, raisins, salad dressings, soy sauce, sunflower seeds, Tabasco, tea, water chestnuts, Worcestershire sauce, canned vegetables, vinegar.

*Refrigerator:* butter or margarine, cheese, cheese spread, cottage cheese, cream, eggs, fruit (inc. lemons and limes), herring tidbits, horseradish, mayonnaise, milk, salami, sour cream, vegetables, whipped topping, whipping cream, yogurt.

*Freezer:* berries (blueberries, strawberries, raspberries), bread (inc. party rye, pita), coffee lightener, cheese (frozen cheese does not slice well, but is excellent for crumbling or grating), hot dogs (cocktail), ice, ice cream, juice concentrates, sherbet.

*Party supplies:* paper cups, plates, napkins (cocktail and dinner size); plastic or foam glasses; plastic flatware; toothpicks, and cloth napkins (no iron) to add a touch of elegance to any party.

*Bar supplies:* beer, bitters, bourbon, brandy, Canadian whiskey, cognac, gin, grenadine, lemons, limes, liqueurs, mixes (Bloody Mary mix, ginger ale, soda, tonic, etc.), rum, rye, Scotch, sherry, soft drinks, vermouth (dry and sweet), vodka.

# Index